CONTROLLED

Susan Finn Alpert

ISBN: 1505891485
ISBN 13: 9781505891485

DEDICATION

This memoir is dedicated to my brother, Jackie, whose sole dwells within my own. I pray I have given him the second chance for a full and ultimately happy life.

To my brother, Gerry, who, as brother and father figure, has guided me throughout my life with lessons of strength, achievement and accomplishment.

To my mother who taught me perseverance even in the darkest of times.

To my children, David, Tracy and Lisa, who have loved me and stood by my side even when I did not deserve it.

To my best friend, Judy, whose compassion and wisdom have been there for me day and night. She was the ultimate matchmaker by introducing me to my partner for life. Her door and her heart are always open.

To the love of my life, my husband, Barry Alpert, who has brought me full circle and taught me the true meaning of love

CHAPTER 1

THE AWAKENING

"Oh my God" was all I could think as I was startled awake, predawn, by a voice telling me "you are me". It was as if he had spoken right into my ear. Somehow, I knew that voice belonged to the brother I never knew. He had drowned at age five, more than three years before I was born. Here I was, 52 years old, and just beginning to grasp who I was, why I was even born, and maybe give reason to why my life had turned out as it did. The room was pitch dark as I bolted awake from a deep sleep. I keenly remember the pounding of my heart and the chill that went through me, and to this day, each time I recall hearing that voice, I experience that same chill. My husband was asleep beside me and there was not another sound in the house. At first, I was frightened at the thought racing through my brain. Then it became the lightning bolt, the moment of truth. The rest of that night, the shock of hearing that voice would replay in and endless loop. As I tossed and turned, my thoughts were spinning. There was no falling back to sleep. I was now wide awake. I felt almost panicky waiting till morning to call my brother, Gerry, to tell him what had happened. What would he think of me? Morning seemed to take forever.

The past is the past, but there is no escape from your beginnings. As I am now 71 years old, I have a story to tell about my life, as strange as it may seem, a life that was begun before my birth.

As I learned growing up, my mother had lost a 5 year old son to a drowning accident. At that time, my parents were living in New Jersey and had two sons ages ten and five. The accident happened at the lake behind my grandparent's home. The house that overlooked the lake was a large, white two story frame home with a big front porch where family often gathered. I remember sitting on that porch, with my cousins, playing in the big rocking chairs. We could play for hours. In the front yard were two beautiful lilac trees, we would climb the trees always appreciating their fragrance all summer long.

Until he passed away, I remember my grandfather living alone in that house with his caregiver. My grandfather was an amputee from world war one. He had lost a leg, above the knee, due to frostbite. He had to get around on crutches, but, nevertheless was the jolliest of men who adored all 14 of his grandchildren. He would have us laughing hysterically when, as we watched, he would quickly push his false teeth in an out of his mouth. He always invited us kids to play in his general store, which was just next to the house. Visits to his store meant fun for us. The store, had lots of penny candy. He would let us be creative and make our own ice cream sundaes. We would scoop whatever flavors we would choose and top the ice cream with whipped cream, sprinkles and cherries. Then we would play pinball for as long as we wanted. We seemed like carefree children. That is all except me.

My grandfather's store and his home overlooked the lake. My memories are a mix of the comfort and fun I was having at the house and store and the fear I was feeling being so close to that lake which symbolized evil. My forbidden lake. This was the very same home where my mom grew up, and the same lake where she and her six younger siblings had played constantly, growing up, during the summer months in New Jersey.

On just such a warm summer day in 1939, my brothers, Gerry and Jackie, were outside playing ball and, while backs were turned, somehow, Jackie disappeared. When they found him, it was just too late.

I learned, many years later from my brother, Gerry, that our mom had slipped into a depression after Jackie's death and he told me, as he recalled, "it seemed she never smiled again until you were born". There was miscarriage after miscarriage until I was born, in a taxi, at 2 AM, during a December blizzard. A healthy baby girl, unaware of the huge burden to be carried on such little shoulders.

My first memory of my life is a flashback which has surfaced almost every day of my life. I am three years old, a little girl shaking with fear, standing in a corner of the hallway that enters the living room and I am watching death. Something isn't right. My father is sitting on the couch. He isn't moving. I wondered if he was sleeping. From another room, I can hear screaming. It is my mother's voice, franticly screaming into the party line phone, "hang up! get off! I need help! I need an ambulance!" I am still shaking in that same corner with my eyes fixed on my father, on the couch, as the house suddenly seems to begin filling with people and commotion. The last part of that flashback is my Aunt Bea putting a red plaid bathrobe around my shoulders. I was so cold and that robe felt so warm. She was holding me close to stop me from shaking, comforting me, and trying to calm me, as she walks me to my bedroom.

CHAPTER 2
THE FLASHBACK

Maybe this is where my story might start... my flashback. I am only three years old. Memories are blurry and sketchy. What I do remember is that my father was suddenly gone. He had died at 39 years old. As I grew up, I remember hearing my mother often tell me to "be a good girl or God will punish you." Did God punish me? Was it something I did that caused my father to die and my family to fall apart? That thought would continually plague me as I grew up.

Traumatized by her own life, my mom tried her hardest to create a home for me and my brother Gerry to grow up in. My brother was only 15 years old and now needed to take over the role of male head of the family. He took over lots of responsibility for mom as well as for me, his "baby sister".

Mom's life had not been easy. As the oldest of 7 children, she was usually held responsible for watching over and caring for all of them. She had lost most of her hearing at age five from a bout of scarlet fever and measles. From then on, she relied on hearing aids the rest of her life. In grade school, children teased and tormented her about those hearing aids. Just one more obstacle, in an already difficult childhood, from which she somehow learned strength, compassion and the ability to persevere.

Now, at age 38, she had suddenly become a widow, with a 15 year old son and a 3 year old daughter. Within the short span of four years, she had lost her 21 year old youngest brother, during the Second World War, her 5 year old son, her mother and now her husband. Life had to go on. She had no choice but to play the hand she was dealt.

So, here we are, this is my home in Roosevelt, New Jersey, a little town not far from the well-known town of Princeton. The community had only 200 homes, most of them attached, as ours was. It was a one story, three bedroom home always tidy and cozy. The living room had many long windows and was full of light. I remember many bookshelves filled with books and records, collected by my father.   There was a player piano and an antique secretary desk along with the antique beautiful drop leaf coffee table.   The sofa and chairs and lamps made the room warm and alive in my memory.   There was an entrance foyer where we kept a big storage chest so that we could protect winter clothing storage with mothballs.   The house had an eat-in kitchen and three bedrooms.   I loved the house I grew up in.   On the back porch, there was a swing for me and the backyard had clotheslines where mom would hang our clothes out to dry.   Weeping willows filled the back yard and bright yellow forsythia bushes brightened the front.   This is the home to which I was brought after birth and lived for the next 18 years.   The home where all those indelible memories began.

How does a three year old deal with such a sudden and profound loss?   I could not comprehend never seeing my father again.   I remember crying for him and searching everywhere for him, as if he was just hiding.   I felt like I searched for him for the longest time.   He was suddenly gone from my life.

I had a puppy, Penny, which my father had given me. She was a toy miniature Doberman Pincher, small enough for me to carry her in my little purse.   She slept in my bed every night and was my constant companion every day.   I was desperately lonely for my father.   Although I was just three years old, his loss caused a pain that was visceral.   I had already begun to see the flashbacks of that last night with him.

Life began to change so quickly. My mother was suddenly going off to work every day. My brother, Gerry, was there for me at home. What I did not have was a concept of exactly how drastically and permanently life was changing. I just could not understand where my father had gone. I wanted every day to be just like before, but no, he never came back to me or my brother or my mom. I wanted my mother to laugh and be happy again. I began to feel, now more than ever, that it would be up to me to bring the happiness into my mother's life. How did all this happen? Maybe I was to blame. Was my father's death because of something I did wrong?

I wish I could share more about him, but I had very few threads of memories and then, over time, even those memories gradually began to fade. You can only hold onto a voice or a song or the feeling of a hug just so long. I could almost hear him singing to me "if you knew Susie like I know Susie." As I grew up, I even doubted if any of my cherished memories were real. Life was so different now.

When my mom started going to work each day, I was being dropped off at her sister's house each morning. I loved my Aunt Bea and she loved me back. She loved to cook and bake. I could stand and watch her for hours.

Walking into her kitchen, there was always a delicious smell. I remember the Tasty Cake treats she kept for us in the corner kitchen cabinet We loved those treats which we got for being good.

Aunt Bea was so pretty and had a heart full of love. Her hair was dark and her eyes were blue, just like my mom's. Except, she had a magical twinkle in her eyes. I had fun being with her and playing with my cousins Annette and Jo Ellen. They became like sisters to me. Annette was three years older than I was and Jo-Ellen was two years younger than me, barely a toddler. As we grew up, we loved playing in out outdoor doll house that was actually a small office. We could spend endless hours playing house with our dolls. Then as we got older, we started playing games... Annette and I had an ongoing game of monopoly set up in the corner of the living room, for what seemed like years. This is the house where I saw the very first television set. My cousins and I were mesmerized by this new invention!

My Aunt always called me and introduced me as her third daughter. She pointed out the fact that I even looked the most like her. My days were filled and I guess I adjusted to this new life.

My Aunt's husband, Uncle Phil, was a difficult personality. A gruff, demanding man, quick to get angry and yell at my Aunt. She had such a sunny disposition and never reacted to his temper more than to say "I'm sorry" and brush away his tantrums as if they never happened. I loved her dearly and learned to mimic her tolerance and warmest of hearts. My uncle never did holler at me or my cousins, but we were always frightened that he could, and so tried to be on very best behavior when he was home. As I look back on my life, I have to believe this was the home life "model" I most closely identified with.

On days when it wasn't convenient for my Aunt to take care of me, I was dropped off at my mother's brother's home, which was just down the street. My Uncle Gil and Aunt Lola were always there for me too. I felt their love completely. At their house, I was with my younger cousins Marty and Robert that I loved like little brothers.

My Uncle Gil was over six feet tall and, in my eyes was as handsome as any movie star. He had been a paratrooper and I remember him teaching me to tie shoe laces on his paratrooper boots. He had those same blue eyes and that same twinkle in those eyes as his sister, my Aunt Bea, and the same sweet loving nature. My Aunt Lola always welcomed me on days I stayed at their home. She amazed me with her talents. Not only was she a wonderful cook, but she had a fabulous singing voice and could play piano and accordion. We children were always entertained.

As I grew up into a teenager, my Uncle Gil was the one who taught me to drive and to perfect my parallel parking skills. I passed my driver's license exam on the very first try. He was very proud of me. Even today, when I parallel park, I can hear his voice telling me when to turn the wheel. I guess I was growing up surrounded by mom's family and feeling totally loved and nurtured.

Mom's other brother and sisters lived in New York and visited with us on weekends. I remember summer weekends meant family barbeques in the back yard at my Aunt Bea and Uncle Phil's house or across the road at Lola and Gil's home. Those weekends meant a menu of London broil, corn on the cob, cole slaw and potato salad. My Aunt Bea always baked the chocolate cake and lemon meringue pie for dessert. We children were always ready to sing, dance and perform for the crowd of Aunts and Uncles. Those were the visits when hearts were light and the air was filled with love and laughter.

As for my father's family, we rarely saw them after his death. I imagine his loss was very difficult for them as well. They were colder personalities, lacking in the fun and warmth of my mom's family. For whatever reason, visits with that side of the family were few and far between. My grandfather was very quiet, and devoutly religious. I cannot remember ever having any conversation with him, but I do remember he had a head-full of white hair, spent hour after hour in prayer and lived well into his nineties. My grandmother on that side had died before I was born. One of my father's sister's, remained single, and live with and cared for my grandfather until his death.

Another of my father's sisters would always join us for special occasions, like graduations, and my wedding day. Her visits were always was a downer for me because she never failed to remind me of the loneliness I must be feeling for my father's absence. She was more right than she even knew, but why did she have to be reminding me? I was trying so hard to keep that loneliness in check.

Still, I felt surrounded by love. However, I was growing up needy. I needed to have everyone loving me. I needed to never have anyone angry with me, and I needed to make everyone happy. I don't remember exactly when it started, but from that time, I never stopped having my intense flashback memory of that night my father died and daydreams of my father coming back to me.

As a little girl, while playing, I had overheard stories about "the tragedy" that had occurred at the lake. Probably I wasn't meant to hear those stories. But little girls hear lots of things not meant for them to hear. The homes of my Aunt Bea and Uncle Gil were close and directly across from my grandfather's house and that very same lake that took my brother.

Throughout all the years I was growing up, I was near that lake almost every day. It seemed to me, that it was huge. The water always looked so dark and all across there were many scattered clusters of water lilies. I could see a dam at the opposite side. Since I would see that lake almost every single day, every day I was drawn to it as I envisioned the nightmare that had occurred. I always had to swallow my fear and blink away my tears. I didn't want anyone to see the truth of what I was feeling. For me, those images of my brother drowning were hypnotic, powerful and gripping. I was constantly drawn to it, and I just wanted to see that lake up close. I never told anyone about these feelings. As a family, no one ever spoke of the drowning but every one of them must have relived it a million times. If I felt such a powerful emotion, I could only imagine what my mother must have felt as she passed that lake each day. Those feelings remained forever unspoken.

Since our home life had fallen apart, I tried, as hard as I could, to be a source of happiness and to make my family smile, laugh and love me. I desperately needed everyone's love to fill the void I was feeling by not having my father there.

I often silently wondered what would become of me if my mom was to die. Who would adopt me? Would my brother take care of me, or my Aunt or Uncle? How or when it started, I don't know, but I felt I had to please everyone to earn their love. These needs became an obsession of sorts. I could not handle anyone being upset with me. I would be overcome with guilt if I made anyone angry. My reality was: If I gave love, I got love in return.

My mother remained overprotective of me. We never went near that lake. My fear of the water began right then and there and continued into my adult life. I was both drawn to get close to the lake, while at the same time having a feeling of terror.

The best one word description of my mom would be genteel. She possessed a warm but quiet nature. She was petite, pretty and always neatly dressed. Her hair was dark, her eyes were a quiet blue. She neither cursed nor drank nor smoked and definitely had a strong set of rules regarding right and wrong. She didn't believe ladies should smoke, drink, wear slacks or ever step out with rollers in their hair, and she cringed knowing that her sisters did it all. Her dress code was always prim and proper, right down to the white gloves she kept in the car. She always wore those gloves when driving at night. Those gloves were for her very precise hand signals in those days before cars had directional signals.

Always serious, yet loving and warm, she did her best to raise me. She was fascinated with the proverbs and taught me every one of them. To my mom, these were the words to live by. In our home, the Golden Rule was paramount: Do unto others as you would have others do unto you. She taught me to always remember the words: people in glass houses shouldn't throw stones, you make your bed and you lie in it and never hang your dirty linen on the line. As her life had been so overwhelmed by tragedy, it was probably easier for her to simply teach these guidelines to me as the rules of life. Not wanting to cause her any more pain but rather to bring her happiness, I felt it was my duty to live by these rules.

Growing up, the lake remained off limits for me, which made it even a more troubling curiosity. During summer months, other families, visiting from New York City, would swim, fish and row boats across the lake. The same lake I was always being kept away from, seemed such a source of fun for others. These were the rules as Mom was intent on my staying safe.

My brother oversaw everything at home. My blond, blue eyed, teenage brother, Gerry, was amazing even then. Although he never signed up for the role of head of the household, at age fifteen, he stepped up to the plate, and did an incredible job caring for both me and mom. I watched as he helped my mom with all her paperwork, and the two of them could talk and problem solve anything together. He quickly became the number one man in my life. Somehow, between the ages of three and eight, through my eyes, my brother became my father. Yes, in my eyes, he was my father. I idolized him. I would go to him constantly for everything from schoolwork to issues with friends.

But, there were things I didn't talk to him or anyone else about, such as the neediness and guilt that was going through my mind, my flashbacks, my fears of the lake or my having an imaginary friend. That was my private world. I think that friend might have been my father, as I was always sharing and loving and never went to sleep without my imaginary friend by my side.

Many of my classmates from Public School in Roosevelt were with me throughout high school years and have continued to be friends throughout my life. Our bonds were strong. Throughout elementary school, my fascination was my "boyfriend", Eddie. Geography aside, between New Jersey and Miami, we remain close friends even today. After we graduated, from elementary and got into high school, our relationship changed. There were no more picnics, parties, kissing games and dancing. We just became good friends. Our horizons were expanding. In High School, he played basketball. I was a cheerleader and he always volunteered to drive me to the games.

My best girlfriend from kindergarten and throughout high school was Iona. She was petite and beautiful, with violet blue eyes like Elizabeth Taylor. From elementary school years until high school graduation, we shared life experiences and visited in each other's houses, as best friends do. Across the miles, she too remains a close friend even today. We share personal and unique remembrances and stories of times gone by. It seems that years and miles of separation do not diminish close childhood bonds or those shared memories.

While friendship and childhood bonds were strong, our world was very sheltered. As children, we rode our bikes together every day. We played jump rope and hop scotch in the never busy streets. We hiked through and played in the woods behind my house. I remember after playing in the woods, always having to have my head and body checked for wood tics. We had roller skates with keys for size adjustments and we skated together before the days of skateboards. On rainy days, when forced to be indoors, we played board games. Those were the days long before computers. We didn't even have television sets yet. We felt protected and safe enough to hitch hike from town to town. On my mom's days off, she would be cooking and cleaning. The house was always neat and clean, and filled with the delicious aromas of whatever she was preparing. There were no security systems or burglar alarms. The milkman delivered milk to our doorstep before the days of supermarkets. Life was easy.

As I grew up, religion was meaningless to me, but my participation made my mother happy and so I participated.

She belonged to an Orthodox synagogue. It happened to be the only synagogue in our little town. For her sake, I attended services on holidays, however, it wasn't at all meaningful for me and I learned nothing. My mom kept a kosher home and lit Shabbos candles every Friday night. It was her ritual and I always joined her although it did not have any profound meaning for me other than to make her happy. None of her brothers or sisters followed any of these religious traditions.

I worked hard in school and made my brother very proud of me. Winning his approval was a must. I was just eight years old when he told me he was getting married. I was so excited. I loved the idea of having a "new sister". I abruptly stopped loving the idea when I realized he would not be living with my mom and me anymore.

I felt abandoned again. I wanted his full attention. I could forget about that and definitely forget about being loved by my "new sister."

Gerry tried hard to keep mom and me as close seconds. But I never settled for being second, although I hated myself for the jealousy I was feeling. I couldn't believe it...I was losing "my father" again.

My heart was breaking, but that was only half the pain. The other half was that I could not make my sister in law love me. This was the very first time I actually felt I was NOT loved by someone. With that realization, I felt physical pain and enormous need for affection. I certainly wasn't perfect. I was only eight years old and I was jealous of their relationship and feeling guilty for my jealousy. This estrangement was something I just had to learn to live with going forward.

My sister in law, Norma, may have done her best to try to be kind, but I always felt estranged. Her parents were always loving to both me and my mom. I think they hoped that my brother would join in their women's clothing store business. They were offering him financial security but he was an entrepreneurial spirit and decided to go out on his own in the risky construction business. A decision that more than paid off in their future.

When mom and I would visit their store, I would find myself waiting outside gazing into the showcase window of the toy store next door. In that storefront window was an amazing four post mahogany doll bed with a white lace canopy and a mahogany dresser beside it. It was the most beautiful doll bed set I had ever seen. Week after week, I would look forward to seeing the beautiful doll bed in that store window.

When the Christmas holidays came around, we were invited to join the Hanukah celebration at Norma's parent's home. Their home was much larger than ours and very warm, friendly and inviting. I remember walking in to the delicious aroma of potato pancakes as we arrived for dinner that evening.

After dinner was over, there was an exchange of presents and one of the biggest shocks of my life. They brought in the mahogany doll bed and dresser. I think my reaction caught everyone's attention and concern. Instead of being thrilled and laughing, I found myself bursting into tears, uncontrollable crying and tears. Why was I so upset instead of overjoyed? I think I just couldn't believe anyone could be that kind to me. I never, in my life, imagined I would ever own that doll bed. I never felt deserving of something that wonderful. I knew I would treasure it for life. That Hanukah, I was eight years old and only parted with the bed itself when I twenty one years old. I gave it to my niece, Amy, when I got married. I never parted with the dresser.

I was nine years old when my nephew, Eddie, was born. He carried my father's name and I became totally obsessed with him. My sister in law did allow me all the time I wanted with him and there was nothing I would rather do than be with him, care for him and play "mom". Thanks to my nephew, this soon became a very happy time of my life.

Over the next several years, when I wasn't with him, my time was filled with schoolwork, ballet, tap and piano lessons. These were the prerequisites for becoming a young lady, according to my mom. I adapted, of course, to my brother living "away" and shared as much of his time as he could or would give me. Caring for my nephew was a great way for me to sublimate the desire I had to be a caregiver, nurturer and to give and get love in return. I felt completely bonded to that child.

My life could be described as overcompensated with love. There was love surrounding me every day. The love of my mom, my brother and my mom's family.

The Aunts and Uncles that cared for me over those years, while my mom was working, never made me feel lacking in any way. I think they went out of their way to always made me feel special. But I knew I was different.

I was the only child I knew who only had one parent. At school, while the class would recite The Lord's Prayer every day, I would always change the words from Our Father to MY Father who art in Heaven. No one ever heard me or knew that I changed the words. Just another of the secrets I kept.

I tried each day to be perfect so that my mom would be happy. She seemed to think everything I did was perfect. When I would test her with my scribbled drawings, she even loved my "art."

My brother was another story. Gerry wanted me to be perfect at everything, really special and the smartest and the best at whatever I did. There was no doubt about the fact that he had huge expectations of me. This was his constant theme as I grew up. He didn't care what I chose to be, but whatever that choice was, I had to be the best. I became terribly disappointed in myself if I couldn't meet his expectations. He was the father figure I was desperately seeking.

Now my path was clearly set, be perfect and please both Gerry and my mother. I remained obsessed with the role of pleasing my loved ones. If I could do that, I could be loved and protected from God's wrath. What a simple formula. Obedience made me safe. All I had to do was to behave, in order to be loved and be protected. This worked for me as a little girl. Of course, life became much more complicated as I grew up.

CHAPTER 3

HIGH SCHOOL

Moving along from the more sheltered years of elementary school, the next step was the high school experience and the new conflicts I would face. I was also changing from a little girl to a woman. My personal pain and the need for affection would reach a peak as I entered high school.

There were now "men" in my life who were seeking my attention and wanting to show affection. My heart was being pulled in many directions. There was my mother, who was constantly trying to protect me as her little girl, who always knew right from wrong. My brother kept the pressure on. He was all about academic achievement and was expecting all A's and excellence in everything I did. Then there were the boys, one in particular, named Justin, who just wanted to have fun. Since my strong suit was as a people pleaser, life was setting me up to fail, to disappoint someone meant to fail. How could I possibly please them all?

Things were changing and life, as I knew it, became much more complicated when I entered high school. The flashbacks and the guilt continued to torment me. My role as people pleaser and achiever, as well as definitions and expectations of love were now much more challenging and I was feeling tremendous emotional turmoil. As I went through the paces, I could feel the pressure mounting. Every day became a source of stress in this tug of war pulling me in too many directions.

Aside from the emotional challenges I was feeling, I have to say there was also a new emotional high. It was becoming a huge challenge to appear to be the little, innocent curly haired, green eyed girl my mother wanted and the A student my brother expected me to be. I was working harder than ever to make everyone happy. I know that I wanted perfection, I wanted it all. I became even more driven to please everyone. I had to work this dilemma out. I studied hard and got the A grades, as expected. I belonged to The National Honor Society, and became a cheerleader. In the marching band, I played the glockenspiel, and in the orchestra I played the xylophone. I sang in the chorus, and was a Class Officer all four years.

This was a very conflicted life, a combination of nerd and rah-rah. It was truly an emotional commotion. Typical to high school behavior, there were always cliques. I refused to join in clique behavior. I tried to befriend everyone. That was not an easy task.

During that time, I also became the freshman girlfriend of the hottest, "bad boy" senior and owner of a black 57 Chevy convertible. For months we had noticed each other, as we passed, in the school hallways and never said more than a casual "hi". Then one Saturday evening, at the weekly high school canteen dance, he came over and asked me to dance. The song they were playing was "Sea of Love" and I could tell he wanted me in a way I had never been wanted before. The chemistry was palpable. Stepping onto the dance floor, I felt the touch of his warm arms around me for the first time ever as my body moved close to his. It was an awakening. That night was my initiation, my first dealings with the incredible turn on of intimacy. I felt transported to a world I never knew existed. My heart was pounding with the sweet expectation of making Justin happy and giving and getting love back from this man.

Since I was only five feet tall and petite, he seemed very tall, and very slim. He had an incongruous nickname of

Chubby. His brown eyes were bedroom eyes, and his kiss was magically warm and sweet. The dancing that night made the evening intoxicating.

For me, dancing became a vital part of those years. An emotional outlet of sorts. From that night on, every time Justin and I were together, I felt that same rush of hormones. I gave him pleasure just by being "his girl". We were a pair of lovebirds in that 57 Chevy convertible.

Even though I didn't drink and didn't smoke, he was happy enough to have a girl whose mission it was to make him happy. He had very strong and often angry demands of my time and of me sexually. As much as I objected, it was a struggle to fight his advances and ultimatums for fear of losing him. What kept us together was my pleasing him in every other possible way. Our hands were never off limits. This was my secret weapon. Make another person happy and love will be there for me.

My perfect outward behavior kept my hidden sexuality a major secret from my mom. My brother was now so busy, in his married life, that he didn't notice what was going on with me. As I look back over those high school years, thankfully I was terrified of becoming pregnant and just as terrified of venereal disease, so sex could go no further than petting. No matter how angry Justin would be with me, I always knew just where to draw the line. I was craving the love of this man, and it was tormenting me to ever have him angry at me. I felt guilty because his anger was definitely my fault. I hated it when anyone was angry with me. This relationship was certainly, as I look back, the training ground for my fascination with "bad boys". It was not only our religious differences, which would break my mother's heart, he was Catholic and I was Jewish, but I also realized that since I had aspirations of college, and he had none, this man could never be "the one" for me.

I was speechless when he wrote in my yearbook: "she is a tree of life to them that lay hold upon her and happy is everyone that retaineth her." When high school was over, I knew my heart might break, but we would separate and I would be moving on into my future. But for the time being, I would not give him up. However, those high school years remained a mix of hard work, secrets, frustration and fun.

Justin and I loved parking, petting, dancing and just being close in each other's arms, any time that was possible. As long as my grades were good, my mom was busy working and never noticed that I had such a healthy teenage libido.

Along with being prim and proper, my mom was also very much a prude. Discussions regarding sex just never came up. She would have kept me in an undershirt forever to avoid discussing a breasts. When the time came that I definitely needed to wear a bra, I went to my Aunt Bea for guidance. She would take care of it and handle her sister. Mom and I never did discuss such subjects as breasts and bras. I grew up right in front of her as she remained in complete denial. She never would have believed the sexuality I was discovering and enjoying day after day.

Justin would drive me home from school. We would share some private petting time together and he would be gone from my house before my mom got home from work. He would leave with just enough time for me to set the table, start dinner and do a little ironing before starting my homework. To mom, I was still that little protected girl who came home every night, did her homework, and got all A's on her report card and lived by those all important proverbs. I have to admit it was a delicate balance keeping my mom and my boyfriend happy. I made certain she saw only the part of me I wanted her to see. So I felt like a great success….I met the challenge and I was pleasing everyone, at least almost.

The truth is, I now had a secret life beyond my flashbacks and fantasies. The only person I could share some of my secrets with was my cousin/sister, Annette. She was almost 3 years older than me. That age difference made her seem worldly. She secretly smoked. Only I knew about that, and was her co-conspirator as I helped clear the smoke out though her bathroom window. She was so pretty and petite with curly blond hair. I wore her hand me downs from childhood till my wedding day. Throughout elementary school we played monopoly every day after school. Throughout high school we shared each other's secrets with faithful loyalty.

Then, the unthinkable happened. One night in 1958, on the first day of spring, there was a freak snow storm. I was about 15 years old and had decided to invite some girlfriends over for a pajama party sleepover that night. My friends and I were laughing and playing games and singing along with records and my player piano, late into the night. In the morning, we all got bundled up in our winter coats, hats, gloves and boots, and made our way to go over to the general store to buy some milk and eggs and bread for our breakfast.

I was surprised to see my Uncle Gil's car heading toward us as we trudged thru the snow that crossed the road to the store. My uncle was still so handsome and collegiate looking. As I said before, in the early years he taught me to tie shoe laces, and at 15 he taught me to drive and made me an excellent parallel parker. He was consistently a loving, wonderful caregiver to me over the years. I loved him dearly.

That blustery cold morning, I vividly remember him pulling over in the car, getting out and kneeling down to talk to me. His words devastated me. "They had a little trouble with Kevin last night". Kevin was my brother's second son. My second nephew, just 6 months old. Then the words: "Kevin died" I was suddenly feeling para-lyzed. I was overcome with grief, and felt as if I might col-lapse. It was as if I was in shock, as I stood there in snow up to my knees. Suddenly, at the same moment, I was overcome with guilt. All that went thru my mind was how *could* I have been having so much fun at the same moment my nephew was dying? How could I have not felt some-thing at that moment? I felt a stunning sense of guilt. It was my fault! I was in high school, living a lie, and once again God punished me.

Now every night I had silent conversations with my fa-ther, as if he could see all, and I would apologize for the "bad" in me. I was constantly craving love and affection. I was a good girl but I was doing bad things. Now my life and lies had caught up with me. The guilt was horrible. I felt as if my bad behavior had killed my nephew as it had probably killed my father. I could always hear my mother's warning voice that if I was bad she didn't have to punish me, because God would. This was just how it happened. This was it!!! How could I ever believe in such a wicked God that just kept taking loved ones away from me?

I felt like I would never stop crying. I went to Kevin's funeral the next day. The day was snowy and bitter cold.

I remember shaking the entire time, thinking and knowing, in my mind, that my actions had caused his death. It was probably one of the most gut wrenching days of my life, adding to my feelings of guilt, and the flashbacks that continued to haunt me.

My nephew, Eddie, was just 6 years old when Kevin died. That day, he would hold me and ask me to please not cry. "Kevin just died, that's all, it will be OK", but it wasn't OK. The funeral for that baby tore my heart out, and haunted me. I had never felt hate before, but now I was hating God!!

The rest of high school finished as a blur. I felt lost. Intimacy became a part of me I hated. I split with my boyfriend and as I tried to turn life around, I was on my way to college to become a nurse. Of course, nurturing, love and compassion were part of every cell of my being, except toward God. I could move on and continue giving my care, love and happiness to others.

CHAPTER 4

COLLEGE DAYS

As I left high school and moved into my college years, life felt like another new beginning. It was as if I was entering a new dimension. I was proud to have been accepted to U Penn Nursing. My mother had always preached about the importance of a woman having a profession. She knew, firsthand, how unpredictable life could be and taught me that I must always have a way to make a living for myself. She also stressed how important it was to start saving and to always set money aside to save. She called it money for a rainy day.

I might have been poor, but I certainly didn't feel poor. I actually looked forward to getting, and loved wearing, hand me down clothes from my cousin, Annette, because

I felt they made me look as pretty as she looked when she wore them. I felt well dressed, I felt smart and I knew I was fulfilling my passion for a great medical education.

My family tells me that from the time I was just a little girl, my life's dream was to study medicine and to nurture and care for the sick. It seems I put a lot of band aids and bandages on my dolls.

The flashbacks of that night and the visions of the lake were always present, and part of my private world, but still, life felt good. I was moving on and it was a wonderful transition. I was on the University of Pennsylvania campus and was still only an hour away from my family. My mom never kept secret her wish that I would come home every weekend. She made her wishes and her loneliness very clear. Her voice did not mask her disappointment when I told her I would not be coming home for a weekend. I was making a choice. I had to study and I had to socialize. I really leaned on my brother to deal with our mom. He agreed that I needed to stay at school and live my life. On those weekends, he would always plan a visit with mom to be certain she was busy.

I met my first of many boyfriends the first week at school. We had both attended the same meeting. He was a freshman from New Jersey. Mal was tall, handsome and smart. We sort of bonded instantly. He remained a constant friend that I dated throughout the years. Mal not only taught me to play guitar, but amazingly never got angry and never pressured me to do more than be his date and enjoy the ZBT fraternity parties. Ours was a platonic relationship. A totally different relationship than what I previously experienced in high school. I was not used to being treated with respect for my feelings. Mal was a "gentleman". I had absolutely no experience with a gentle man. Our friendship was strong, but I was not feeling that physical attraction that I had felt for Justin in high school.

I still did not smoke, and I still did not drink. In fact, I hated the taste of alcohol. At fraternity parties, I would carry around a glass of scotch just for show. I only knew how to order scotch because it was my brother's drink of choice. I never touched it. Mal and I certainly had fun together over four years, but that magical chemistry was missing.

I dated many other men over those years at Penn. I didn't know it then, but recognize now that the problem was that they were all were too nice to me. The strong tempered male that dominated his woman, was the role model I most identified with. Ridiculous as it seems now, that is what got my attention. The superficial social life was great fun, but for some reason that emotional connection, that "special feeling", which I imagined to be sexual attraction, or love, or feeling fulfilled was always missing. When I felt like a relationship could develop, I would seek intimacy. I would feel that need to please my date, but never felt any sense of pleasure of my own. The kisses and caresses were a one way street. I know I really tried to experience sexual fulfillment, but never reached or even came close to it. There were many wonderful men that I dated and spent periods of time with over those years. Along with a business student from Dartmouth, I dated several medical students, a dental student at Penn, two ophthalmology residents, a Urology resident and even a Psychiatry resident, all from Penn. They were all wonderful men who would have made great partners for someone, but not for me. I could never again feel that rush of hormones I had felt with Justin. Believe me, I tried to get it back, but I still felt like a part of me was missing or altered. I recognized that I was having major intimacy and sexuality problems.

That magical chemistry I had felt in my high school relations no longer existed. Thoughts of sex brought on thoughts of guilt. As hard as I tried to let it go, I must have had either God's wrath or my mother's morality entrenched in the back of my mind, because those guilty thoughts prevailed and overpowered any sexual satisfaction.

By this stage of my life, I began to know that I could no longer change what made me tick. Well, maybe I could have accomplished that with lots of psychotherapy, but I had none of that. I was simply numb when it came to men. Any arousal I felt came from discipline and punishment, which began with my high school relationship. I knew, in a male partner for life, I would need that chemistry. I also needed humor and brains. This would prove the ultimate set up for the perfect storm which was yet come.

When I finally reached the end of my senior year, I was totally enthralled with the medical education, and decided I wanted to re-enroll into the Medical School. My grades were good enough that all I needed was to complete a few prerequisite courses and I would be in. I was psyched!!

During the spring break of my senior year, my mother took me on a vacation to Miami Beach. The afternoon we arrived, as mom was unpacking, I decided to take a walk and check out the area close to our hotel. I was not outside walking more than a few minutes when a convertible with five boys pulled over to the curb. The driver called out "I think I know you from somewhere", obviously a pick up line, but I called back "no, just a first time visitor". He pulled his car up to the curb, said he would like to get to know me and show me around. He said his friends were just leaving. That struck me as a bold move by this young man. He was obviously bold and aggressive. I said if he met my mother and she approved and agreed, I would love to be shown around. His name was Barry.

As it turned out, when I told him I was a nursing student at Penn, Barry said he was a medical student at the University of Miami. I'm not sure why I didn't trust him, but I didn't believe him, so I quizzed him on the anatomy of the kidney. The kidney was the most difficult anatomy I could come up with. I was shocked when he knew all the answers! It was quickly obvious to me that this young man was very smart, and also, obviously, very bold.

He came over to meet my mother, who, to my surprise, approved of my going off with him for a couple of hours to see the sights. We did just that. We toured the beach in his old beat up convertible. His looks were inviting, especially the color of his eyes. At five foot seven, he was tall to me. His hair was dark. He wore dark rimmed glasses and his eyes were blue green. We talked, and we laughed. Now, I was seeing that Barry was smart, funny and bold. Or was it controlling? I realized he didn't ask what I would like to do, but rather told me what he wanted to do. What was it about his being strong willed and dominant that got my attention?

During that week, I think he visited with me, on the beach, every day we were there. He and I shared lots of good conversation, and lots of laughs, maybe a few kisses that could have led to more, but did not. After all, this was simply an isolated vacation week. When the time came to say goodbye, we did so without even exchanging phone numbers. Those were the days of expensive long distance phone calls. Therefore, it was just a hug and a kiss good-bye, with no thoughts of ever meeting again.

Early in June of my senior year, I found a note in my mailbox which read: "Barry from Miami is in town and wants to get together." There was a phone number, so I called him. What a surprise! He said he was going to be in Atlantic City for the summer, working as a beach doctor. He wanted me to come visit him the upcoming weekend. I agreed. Now looking back, I realize he didn't ask if I would like to visit him, but rather he told me he wanted me to come to Atlantic City.

When the weekend came, I was finding myself quite excited to see him again. And when he met me at the bus, I was sure I had made the right decision to join him for the weekend. For the first time in years, suddenly I felt that chemistry! Every type of chemistry! We explored the boardwalk, we explored each other's minds and bodies and found complete compatibility and satisfaction. Yes indeed, he was smart, he was funny, he was sexy and he had an unusually strong personality. This was the very first time, since high school, the chemistry was back!

The strong personality, now that I look back, was the father figure personality. Strong discipline, which seemed to be just what I needed to punish me for all the guilt I had collected throughout my life. He was always telling me how

I could make him happy and please him. Those words were my magic formula. It worked for me and we just seemed to have that chemistry that made it click. That summer, I had perhaps five or six weekends off when I traveled by bus from Philly to Atlantic City to be with him. As summer came to an end, it was sad, but we both were prepared to say "goodbye" again and head back to our own personal pursuits.

A week later a letter arrived and a day later a phone call. Barry wrote that if I would not agree to come to Miami and marry him, I would never hear from him again. That was the first ultimatum. His phone call further explained that I would work while he went thru Med School, then he would work to put me thru med school. He said I would have to postpone my dream, but just for a few years. His exact words were "it is a shame that a mutual love of medicine could part us forever."

He told me he wanted me to fly to Miami, meet his family and make my decision. That is exactly what I did. Barry's family was warm and welcoming. His parents could not have been nicer or warmer toward me. His older brother "jokingly" told me it was a good thing he met a girl from out of state because no girl from Miami, who knew him, would ever consider marrying him. His reputation was that bad. His sister, Bobbi, was fun and smart and I knew we would bond right from the start. I was very much in love with Barry and it all seemed like a natural fit.   He had proposed to me when I arrived, and by the time I left for home, I had accepted his proposal.

CHAPTER 5
WEDDING BELLS

It was a wedding planned hurriedly in order to be convenient for Barry's class schedule. We had arranged to marry. It was December, 1963, Christmas break of his Freshman Year in Med School. That vacation was only two months away from the date we became engaged. By that date, we would have known each other less than six months. We had lived apart except for those five or six weekends we had spent together in Atlantic City. We had never talked about marriage, religion, children or any of the things which couples learn about one another before choosing marriage. We barely knew one another, but our love chemistry was strong. The wedding was quickly approaching.

Barry arrived in New Jersey the Thursday before our Sunday wedding. He and his mother, father, sister, brother, sister in law and brother in law all drove down in one car. It was a sight to see them arrive, all piled into what resembled a circus car. I had met all the family during my October trip to Miami, when I became engaged to Barry. However, no one from my family, of course, had met anyone from Barry's family, and only my mother had ever met Barry.

First order of business was that we quickly apply for our marriage license. With the help of my brother's live-in housekeeper, Lizzie, who came to the courthouse with us, and swore she had known Barry "since that child was in diapers". The most tender and warm hearted, big bosomed Lizzie had been living in at my brother's home for about 12 years by that time. Lizzie deserves a book unto herself. She was love personified and pretty much ran the show at their house. The housekeeping part was purely secondary to her, but her main role was the care of the three children. She had the most gentle hands when it came to caring for them, or for my sunburn on beach days, but her major skill was her "way with words" or shall we call it "storytelling." With Lizzie as our witness, we were given the license to marry. We spent the next two days doing a lot of introductions and last minute wedding planning. We were right on schedule.

Sunday rolled around quickly, and I awoke in a panic of self-doubt, guilt and absolute paralyzing fear, but there was no turning back. As I would be leaving all family behind and moving to Florida, I was in a state of profound sadness because of my father's absence, and my mother's loneliness as I moved so far away. My brother, aunts and uncles all offered me reassurance that they would be close by her.

The day had come. It was a bitter cold December, New Jersey Sunday. I was wearing the hand–me-down wedding gown which had looked so beautiful on my cousin Annette, at her wedding, only a few years earlier. I kept hoping that I looked as pretty as she had. In honor of my wedding, I had the very first manicure of my life which remained a lovely memory until my next manicure twenty years later.

At the ceremony, it was my brother who gave me away. It was impossible for either of us to hide the emotions or hold back the tears. My nephew, Ed, was now 11 and became our Junior Best Man, my niece, Amy, then 3 years old, was my beautiful flower girl. Lizzie brought over my youngest nephew, Jeff, who would turn one year old the following week. I never imagined I would ever live so far away from the family I loved so much. Somehow it happened. I had never imagined the children would grow up without their Aunt Suzie always being nearby and sharing their lives. Suddenly the awakening and now I realized that was exactly what was happening, and I was heartsick.

Classmates and cousins were my six bridesmaids all dressed in green. All of my Aunts, Uncles and cousins were there to help celebrate the occasion. My Aunt Lola chose and sang our wedding song, Fly Me To The Moon, as we stepped onto the dance floor as husband and wife. That was the first and last time we ever danced. I loved to dance. Dancing had been a vital part of my life growing up, but Barry hated to and refused to ever dance again. I guess I was to learn that was rule #1.

So, December 22, 1963, I became Mrs. Barry. It was a heart wrenching feeling to leave my entire family behind as we got into the car and began the drive south to Florida. I felt guilty leaving my mom. She kept saying how happy she was for me, but I could read in her blue eyes the emptiness she was feeling. I was heartsick leaving my brother, as he had become the number one man in my life, until that day, and now I was supposed to have given my heart to a new #1 man in my life. I could hardly bear leaving my niece and nephews, and in fact, at that moment I felt as if I had lost my glow and all my own hopes and dreams. I knew this was not how a new bride should be feeling. My mother's famous proverbs were always with me. This time, all I could think of was: you make your bed and you lie in it. Was it guilt? Had I made the right choice? I certainly didn't know, but, if possible, the flashbacks and the profound loneliness continued to plague me even more.

As Barry and I drove away from the wedding and headed south, I kept myself calm by reassuring myself that this was only a temporary feeling and, indeed, after all, I was very much in love and invested in Barry's medical education. Those were my feelings. I was intensely in love and intensely lonely as we drove south from New Jersey to Florida in the Dodge Dart convertible my mom had given us as wedding gift. Our first night as a married couple was spent in a motel we found in Cherry Hill, New Jersey. We were so anxious to get into the room, we discovered the next morning that we had left the key in the door.

When we arrived in Miami, we immediately moved into the married dorms of the University of Miami and I got a job at South Miami Hospital in the Emergency Room. I took my Florida Nursing boards and passed, so I could work, earn the money to support us and dedicate my time to my husband. Living with a man, and being a wife were two brand new roles for me.

I was totally unprepared to understand the working relationship of a marriage, as I had only lived in a home with one parent. The other role model were my Aunt and Uncle and the stormy side of marriage. He screamed and she laughed it off. He was abusive and she was apologetic. This is what I knew a relationship to be. We had a bit of a bumpy road until I learned "the rules", Barry's rules of marriage. He explained to me, from the start, that marriage was "a benevolent dictatorship". He clearly had defined the roles for the wife. Aside from my full time nursing position, I would do all the grocery shopping, all the cooking, all the cleaning, all the laundry and this list definitely included taking out the garbage. He also hated make up and cologne and I was not allowed to wear either. His rules were iron clad. Not a chance of modifying them. Although I was working full time, I am sorry to confess, his rules worked for me. I did my best to get everything done and not disappoint him. Pleasing him was paramount. Disappointing him meant facing his temper, a temper I had never seen before. Had I found my father figure in my husband? I was now learning about self-flagellation for feeling guilty if ever I let my husband down. I loved him completely even if he would emotionally punish me for forgetting to do any little chore. Maybe I even punished myself more due to guilt and failure to please. It seemed I was always the guilty one. I was the source of any problem.

He was never physically abusive, but certainly was emotionally abusive. He would be furious with me if he didn't have all his needs met. If he ran out of cigarettes, I was responsible, even though he was the only smoker. He would scream and have me leave the house at 11PM, if needed, to go to the store to buy cigarettes. I don't really know if the term Domestic Violence had even been coined back in 1963, but now I recognize that I was definitely a victim. The emotional abuse was unrelenting and something I just had to learn to tolerate.

I was really learning the rules of being of a wife. Well, his wife, at least. I was the only one that EVER had to say the words I'M SORRY. Our married friends had different life styles, and often commented to me about how unbalanced our life seemed. I was so certain that our love affair was more important than any life style adjustment, that their comments never phased me. I was secure in his love, regardless of the style in which he showed it.

I wrote lots of letters to my family and called my mom at least once a week for a three minute conversation. The phone call was a very expensive treat just to hear her voice. I cherished those brief calls as well as her letters. Besides working and running our little home life, while Barry studied, we managed to continue our love affair and have fun with each other and our new circle of friends. For me, I simply never spoke about but never stopped having those flashbacks, and feelings of guilt.

I wish Barry could tell his version of our story going forward, but that is not possible. You will just have to hear my voice, my version, but telling the story is what is important to me. Barry had found in me a girl, a nurturing woman and a workaholic. I was certainly an obsessive compulsive, guilt ridden, people pleaser, with intense flashbacks and profound loneliness. I was controlled from within and from without. I was in need of a father figure for the punishment I felt I had always deserved. I was this girl and I was intensely in love with him. I was never going to totally please my husband. I was a woman always on the brink of being "perfect", but never quite there.

It was not more than a couple of months working in the hospital emergency room, that the plastic surgeon, I often assisted, asked me to come work for him as his office nurse and operating room assistant. Barry was as proud as I was, because Dr. T. J. Baker was a highly regarded professor, teaching hand surgery at the University of Miami. This was a very prestigious job offer. Not more money, still a $4000.00 a year salary, but one of the best jobs I ever have had. We actually moved to the apartment behind Dr. Baker's medical office mansion and tended the grounds in exchange for the apartment rent. Now it was the spring of 1964. Barry would not be graduating until 1966, so we were set with housing and work and our mutual love for medicine as well as our love for each other that held such promise for the future.

CHAPTER 6
INCREDIBLE GRIEF

Now at age 22, having lived almost my entire life with these flashbacks and the haunting memories of that lake, I was still determined to keep them secret and just deal with them and my crazy obsessions for perfection and love. Barry's love, along with his horrible temper and role as my disciplinarian seemed just what I deserved for the guilt I was carrying.

The years I worked with the plastic surgery practice were wonderful work years for me. This was not a cosmetic surgery practice, but rather we cared for trauma patients from auto accidents, burn disfigurement, machinery caused hand trauma and even sex change surgery.

We did about twenty per cent cosmetic surgery which was the "fun" stuff.   I worked in the operating room, in the office, and made weekend hospital rounds for the docs. I was loving it.   I was loving studying medical textbooks alongside my husband, living vicariously through him and dreaming about "my turn".   We had cultivated friendships.   We loved, we played and we studied together.   I had adjusted to my professional responsibilities and to my role as wife.

I was totally blindsided by what came next.   As Barry looked forward to graduation in 1966, he broke the news to me that there would be no medical school for me.   Of course, we argued about how unfair he was being.   I was emotionally devastated by his betrayal.   He had slammed the door in my face.   He had taken my dreams and flushed them.   I had fulfilled my part of the promise and he was totally reneging on his.   Neither my grief nor my tears meant anything to him.   There was no way to win an argument with him.   His decision was final!   He demanded that I stop birth control, become pregnant and start our family.

Just like that, with those words, my dream came to an end, and as he demanded, so did the discussions.   I was totally crushed.   I was totally shocked.   I was heartbroken, hurt, and furious all at the same time.   Yet in my mind, I was powerless.   Where could I go? There was nothing more I could say. What could I do about what was happening? I felt I had no choice other than to as he said and begin another path, another dream. In my heartbroken state of feeling lied to and unfulfilled, I rationalized that I would let motherhood fill the emptiness of my dream to become a doctor.

I was forced to rationalize. I was a woman. I had a husband and, of course, I had planned on having babies some-day. I was just moving that date up a few years. After all, we had already been married for four years and many of our friends were starting families. I just needed to shift my plans. This was not what I bargained for. This was a major shift in plans.

I was quite shocked, and found that I was both amazed and delighted to become pregnant the month after stopping the pill. Barry was proud and felt this was perfect timing for us as we would have our baby in March and be ready to move away for Barry's internship in New York which would begin July first.

Indeed it was a radical shift in plans and dreams, but nevertheless became a thrilling transition to be carrying a baby. My doc really surprised us by announcing he was pretty certain I could be carrying twins. This supposition was something he determined by the growth measurements he kept monthly. That was indeed an exciting possibility.   So much so, I even ordered twin insurance from the local department store.   I was working full time with the plastic surgeons, feeling the glow of pregnancy and becoming totally excited with the prospect of motherhood.

Then, one day in February, just like that, the dream shattered.   My brother had become an important figure in the commercial real estate world.   He would always be my #1 man and father figure although I could never be with him more than maybe once a year.   That week, I knew my brother would be in Miami for a business meeting on Friday.   I was at work, but left messages everywhere to get his number so that we could make a plan to see each other.   By the end of that busy day, there had been no calls or messages.   I learned he had come to Miami, but his schedule was tight and there had been no time for a call or much less a visit.   I was shattered.   I actually became hysterical with heartbreak.   I was so lonely for him that it was an inconsolable sadness.   There was a profound moment of truth when every cell takes on the pressure of loneliness, guilt and punishment.   At that moment, I was eight months pregnant.   I had been thrilled with the life that stirred inside me, kicking, playing and loving me loving it.

Then, just as in previous times in my life, tragedy struck out of the blue.   This emotional turmoil began on Friday and by Monday I knew my baby had stopped kicking.   I rushed to my doctor's office on Monday and was told not to worry, "these things happen", and there was nothing we could do but wait.   Perhaps it was just a change in fetal position.   In those years, there were no tests to be done to confirm anything.   I was sent home to wait.

I continued working and said nothing to anyone, not to the patients, of course, but not even to my family, about what was happening.   Although silently, while my heart was breaking, I continued working and waiting for two more weeks until finally I went into labor.

I remember feeling numb and shocked at what was happening as I checked into the hospital.   When the doctor came in to examine me, his first words were "I think we both know that the prognosis is poor".   Under anesthesia, I could hear the words that my son was stillborn and I could feel my heart breaking with silent sobs that seemed to take my breath away.   My heart was shattered.   That word stillborn would pierce my heart like a bullet, creating a hole that would never quite heal.

Once again in my life, a hole in my heart that could never heal and maybe only be patched.   Barry appeared totally insensitive.   He refused to allow me to have any sort of a service for our son.   He forced me to sign some release papers and that day he took me home, from the hospital, empty handed.   I was drained and emotionally empty. As I was battling depression, or the closest to it I could imagine, Barry insisted I just move on and forget about "it". He said we would have so much fun making another baby.

I had been anticipating the July move to New York with Barry and our new baby and therefore, at work, I had been in on the interviewing process and the subsequent hiring of Jackie, the nurse who replaced my position with the plastic surgery practice. She became a pivotal person in my life as the future unfolded.

To keep from going crazy, I forced myself to go back to work immediately. I quickly replaced my job with a position in the Operating Room at Bascom Palmer Eye Institute for the remaining months until graduation. It was the perfect job for me as I battled depression. I was able to wear a mask to cover my sadness, and I did not have to make small talk.

As we all celebrated Barry's achievements and graduation from Medical School, I hid my feelings of depression and the deception which he had led me to over all those years. We were moving on.

CHAPTER 7
NEW YORK, 1966

And so it happened, Barry graduated, we left Miami and moved to New York to begin his internship. I was leaving behind all my hopes and dreams for medical school as well as the baby that I was supposed to have in my arms to give my life new meaning. I was determined to fight the depression I was feeling and get a job at Maimonides, the same hospital where Barry was interning. I was grieving so many losses: my father, my dreams for medical school and my baby boy. It seemed one of the lowest points in my life up until then. Regardless, we were moving forward.

We found a small one bedroom apartment in a building almost directly across the street from the hospital, at 950 49th Street in Brooklyn, and began the year with hard work and the "fun" of trying to make a baby again.   It wasn't proving to be fun for me and with Barry's grueling internship schedule, he was finding scheduled sex a major inconvenience to his busy internship schedule. When I would call him to come home because of the calendar or temperature guidelines, he would yell at me that he could not tell his resident that he had to go home to screw his wife.

Month after month came the disappointment of not being pregnant despite all my valiant efforts with calendars, thermometers and pillows.   Strollers and carriages were everywhere. It seemed that everyone had a baby except me. We did add to our family with a four month old German Sheppard puppy that my Aunt Lola had to give away.   We named her Cookie.   Our timing was lousy, but after she tore open the only furniture we had ever purchased, we had her trained and she turned out to be incredibly obedient and very protective pet over the next eight years.

One day, faced with the letdown of yet another month not becoming pregnant, I was stricken with despair, almost to the point of hysteria.   I went to my gynecologist's office by taxi because I was crying too hard to drive. Certainly something was wrong with me that caused me to be unable to conceive again. He reassured me of my good health and advised throwing away calendars, pillows and thermometers and just enjoy sex by relaxing with my husband and a glass of wine. His thought was that I was just too uptight and stressed to conceive. Amazing how right he was. By the very next month, I was pregnant

At this point, I want to share a funny story. When I sent the urine pregnancy test to the lab to check for a positive or negative, Barry said if it was negative we would go out for steak and if it tested positive we would go out for lobster. When he brought the lab test result back to me, on the outside he had written "It's a Lobster"!!! I was jubilant, and we went out to celebrate my pregnancy over a lobster dinner!

I began to normalize and glow in the knowledge that soon we would have our baby. We were both very excited and although our work schedules were extremely busy, earning two paychecks, we did the best we could finding some time to enjoy life in New York.

Truthfully, to the best of my ability, I kept my fears hidden, as I always did. As the months passed, I became increasingly terrified that I could lose another pregnancy. That fear of having another stillbirth continued to haunt me along with my hidden flashbacks, guilt and neediness. Barry continued to be tough on me. I was doing my best to recover from my lost dream of medical school and my lost baby, but throughout the pregnancy, Barry remained relentless as far as his temper and his punitive behavior.

A sad but telling example was the night I came home from work in the operating room, seven months pregnant, and prepared his favorite dinner of fried chicken, cole slaw and potato salad.   I had gotten paper plates as friends had suggested to me that using paper plates made life so much easier. We had no dishwasher. When Barry came in from the hospital and saw the dinner on paper plates, he threw everything on the floor and told me to clean up, and start over!   He never wanted to see paper plates used again!! I was horrified to have disappointed him to the point of rage.

I did as he said and this time, I felt I had learned my lesson well and with a determination to try harder to never let him down again.   That was Barry. He loved me.   I knew that. He just had rules that I would have to learn. This incident foreshadowed the years ahead.

Up until May 24th, I was working in the newborn nursery at Maimonides taking care of 30 babies every day. Then, at long last, on the Thursday morning of May 25th, I went into labor. I called the hospital to let the nursery know I would not be in to work but soon would be sending them an admission. At 9:05 AM, our son David was born.

He was a perfect five pounds seven ounces.   I counted fingers and toes.   He was such a beautiful baby.   There are no words to describe the moment of transition into motherhood for me, parenthood for us.   We were both so happy.   It was a miracle.   It was a dream come true.   I felt I could see into the future as I held my son in my arms.

Within five weeks, the internship would be finished and we would be moving from New York to Oklahoma, headed to Tinker Air force base where Barry would become a general medical officer with the rank of captain.   Our road trip was an adventure and having our baby boy with us made it a dream for me.   We arrived in San Antonio for Barry's basic training.   While nursing David and involved with the transition, without giving it a thought, I was shocked to discover I was pregnant again.   I was thrilled!   I felt as if I had hit the Jackpot!   Those next 9 months went by in a blink.   Our daughter, Tracy, was born on Thursday July 18th, at 11:26PM, at the Tinker air force base hospital, weighing in at four pounds twelve ounces.   She was perfect, beautiful and an angel of a baby.   When I took her home the next day she only weighed four pounds nine ounces, tiny, but healthy and strong.   According to our doctor, she was the smallest but the strongest baby in the nursery.   I was certainly feeling fulfilled taking care of my two babies.

We were living on the Air force base in Oklahoma City. I was as happy as I had ever been and the promise of my beautiful family made life feel perfectly complete. Now, I felt as if I was born to be a mother and now discussed my new dreams of having four children. Barry put his foot down. There would be only two. End of discussion. That was the story of my life. I was not allowed to have a dream of my own, so I decided to just be thankful for the blessings of my son and my daughter.

Those years were good years for me and my babies, but the two years in the Air Force serving as a Captain and a General Medical Officer were a struggle for Barry. He resisted as many of the military rules and regulations as he possibly could. However, he did enjoy the inexpensive flying lessons. I took the ground school classes with him and struggled to correct him as he balked at following rules, even the checklist of rules before getting into and flying the plane.

His first solo flight was terrifying. I stood with the instructor at my side, as Barry took off. On his third missed approach landing, I remember Mr. Walky looking at my face full of fear, and telling me "don't worry, we can always shoot him down." Fourth attempt, and finally, he landed the plane.

When Barry and I went out for a flight, I would leave "in case of emergency" notes with the babysitter. I never stopped praying that we would get back home safely from those flying outings. It not only seemed risky, but ridiculous to fly from Oklahoma to Texas for a Pizza. It was just never fun flying with Barry, but going with him was a better choice than facing his wrath if I refused to go.

His non-observance of the rules was hallmarked by our flight from Oklahoma to Miami for vacation. He forgot to file the mandatory flight plan. I had lied and told my mom we were taking a commercial flight. She was terrified of my flying with Barry. We set off for Miami and had the children and the dog with us.

The little Mooney plane was cramped and the cockpit was very noisy. The dog was so frightened, she was constantly scratching at the window to get out. As it turned out, my mother had somehow caught on to my story about flying commercial and called Barry's family in Miami. They called the air base and no one at the base could track our trip because he had not filed a flight plan. Our parents were frantic. It took four days to get to Miami because of bad weather forcing us to land and spend four overnights along the way. Finally we landed in Fort Lauderdale. I think I had prayed to any God who would listen to my prayers and could get us to land safely. Barry was sharply reprimanded when we finally did land at the Florida airbase both for failing to file the flight plan and secondly for failing to even ask permission from the tower before landing. Our vacation only had two days left before we had to pile back into that plane and fly back to Oklahoma.

My husband's temper only exacerbated the guilt I was feeling.   I was still struggling to be the perfect wife and mother.   Over all these years, the flashbacks were there every day of my life.   They controlled and tormented me and yet I never told anyone about them nor could I make them stop.

We survived the two years in the Air Force, and the time went by so fast.   From Oklahoma we moved to Chicago for Barry's Ophthalmology residency at Cook County Hospital.

CHAPTER 8
CHICAGO

The move to Chicago for Barry's residency, actually began with a pre-requisite three month course in Philadelphia. Barry had to complete this mandatory requirement at the University of Pennsylvania, my old stomping grounds. As luck would have it, his discharge from the Air Force prevented him from starting the course on time. Fortunately, I was able to attend and sit in his place for the first month. Each morning, I took the babies with me and they stayed in the nursery provided at the hospital. I had arranged a schedule to work in the Operating Room and also sit in on Barry's required courses.

We got a short lease for a Brook Tree apartment near my mom in New Jersey. Being back in New Jersey was heaven for me. I had my babies, my family, my dog, Cookie, and continued medical education. In addition, it was a brief but wonderful opportunity for David and Tracy to enjoy being with their grandmother as well as my brother and his family. It was a wonderful interlude for me to feel, and be, at home with family. There were children's movies at the pool in the evenings and swimming every day.

When Barry arrived in New Jersey, he took over his classroom work and I continued my hospital job. The three months went by way too fast. I felt motherhood had become my calling. I was still plagued with the same struggles to be perfect and the guilt for failing perfection, and those daily flashbacks of that horrible night my father died. I was learning to accept the strict disciplined life I had with Barry and make the most of it, without complaint. My guilt kept me in tow. Just as he was for me, he was also a strict disciplinarian for the children.

October rolled around much too quickly. We sadly, had to say goodbye to family. We packed our car and set off for Chicago and were now ready to begin the final part of his training. We had pretty much decided we would be moving back to Miami, at the conclusion of his residency, to set up his practice.

When we arrived in Chicago, we found an apartment on Farwell Avenue, on the north side of the city, almost at the Evanston border. It was a 3 floor walkup. We were on the second floor. We were about a half block from the park and Lake Michigan. David and Tracy had just had their first and second birthdays. Moving to Chicago in October was an eye opener. The chill was setting in. I thought I knew what winter was like, having grown up in New Jersey, but none of us was prepared for Chicago style weather. My hand me down wardrobe hardly matched the sub -zero temps, neither did the hand me down wardrobes for the children. Only our German Sheppard didn't seem to mind the weather. We avoided the exposure as much as we could. Luckily, we had a garage for the car. This still required setting an alarm and going down to start the car midway thru the night to insure it would start in the morning. This was only slightly easier than removing the battery, wrapping it in a blanket and taking it into the building's basement. Finally, we resorted to the electric oil dipstick. This was winter in its most extreme form.

Summers were no picnic either as temps climbed into the 100s Since we had no air conditioning, sometimes we just climbed into a bathtub with cool water to lower our body temps. Enough about weather, because when it wasn't boiling or freezing, we loved what Chicago had to offer. My nephew, Ed, was at the University of Chicago, so

I did get to see more of him and even have him come live with us for a short while. It was a treat to have him nearby. I had always enjoyed being in his company from the time he was born. For me, any time spent with him was positive time.

Chicago seemed to have so much to offer. The theaters, the ethnic restaurants, like Chinatown and German Town, the parks, the zoo, the cultural arts provided free by the library system and children's street theater. My children were the joy of my life. David never seemed to take much notice of his little sister until the day she crawled into the playroom and toppled the elaborate structure of blocks he had built. The first words out of his mouth were: "how long will she be staying with us?" When I answered that she will be with us forever, he processed that information with complete and utter disbelief.

As the children were growing up in Chicago, I was as content as I had ever been. Motherhood was totally fulfilling. One day as I picked up Tracy and exclaimed how adorable she was, she said she knew she was adorable, but that David was the smart one! David was obsessed with learning to read and Tracy just loved to cuddle in my lap and have me read to her. I never realized that she didn't understand that her brother was one year older and therefore able to know more than she knew. With that in mind, I enrolled them in a Montessori preschool for the last spring session that we lived in Chicago, so they each could excel in their individual strengths.

I had my bike with two children's seats and, weather permitting, we were out and about as much as possible. With the children secured in their seats and my German Sheppard, Cookie, running alongside the bike, we rode the paths along Lake Michigan. The children loved playing in the park and catching Monarch butterflies with nets, only to let them go and watch in amazement as they flew away. Being with and raising my children was so much fun, all the troubles of my life seemed to disappear.

We were living on a shoestring budget which added even more tension to our family relationship. We were saving every penny we could toward a trip we were planning. Barry wanted to travel through Europe before opening his practice. Those were the days it was possible to travel through Europe for $5 a day, like the book by the same name proposed. We saved every penny we could. I even took unused food back to the grocery for a refund. The savings added up.

July, 1972, the residency was over and I was the first to leave Chicago with the children. We packed all our belongings into the car and I drove, with the kids and the dog, to New Jersey, where I left our car and our dog with my cousin, Jo Ellen, kissed my family goodbye and flew off to Luxemburg with David and Tracy. That summer, David had just turned five and Tracy was about to turn four as we traveled through Germany in July.

By bus and train, the kids and I somehow traveled to the Daimler Benz Mercedes factory in Germany, to pick up our car and drive it back to Luxemburg in time to meet up with Barry. Traveling in a foreign country in a new car with two little children in seatbelts in the back took all the courage I could muster up. I clearly remember the nightmare of the Audubon. It was terrifying! Cars were passing me driving at speeds over 100 miles an hour as I was passing exit signs I could not even read. We finally, amazingly, made it back to Luxemburg where we were picking up Barry and where our adventure continues.

For three months we traveled through Germany, France, Spain, Switzerland, Italy, Yugoslavia and Greece. We survived on the tightest of budgets. Daily, we ate picnic style with bread and cheese and fruit. These were the staples available each day. We slept in youth hostels, on rooftops, in the car and even slept on the beaches in the Greek Islands. We got a modest hotel room once a month to really shower and "refresh". It was a trip we never again could have duplicated. It was the trip of a lifetime and the children were amazing. They obliged us with the best behavior you could imagine from children that age.

Three months and ten thousand miles later, we flew back home to the USA and had our car shipped. The kids and I stopped in New Jersey, picked up our dog and our other car, kissed our family members goodbye once again and drove to Miami very ready to settle down and set up Barry's practice. Before we found an apartment, we stayed with Barry's parents and I took an immediate position in the operating room of a nearby hospital.

The journey continues, as do the flashbacks and the loneliness and the guilt, worthy of the punishing discipline my husband never ceased to bestow upon me.

CHAPTER 9
MIAMI

It was November, 1972, we were back in Miami and the new office building was almost ready. We found an apartment near Kendall Drive and enrolled David in Kindergarten and Tracy in Pre K. We were very involved in work, setting up the practice and finding a home, all at the same time.

While the medical office was readying completion, we began house hunting and found a "handyman's special" house. We were looking for and found the house we could afford in the best public school district, which was much more important than the condition of the house. We borrowed a few thousand dollars from my mother and were able to finance a 90% mortgage. This was the least expensive house in the best school district, and walking distance to the office.

Transitions can probably be tough on any couple or family, and given the temperamental powder keg of our love, we were no exception. Because the cost outside the air force was exorbitant, Barry had to give up flying planes. He decided his hobby would now be sailing.

Having been sheltered from water for most of my life, I now had to bite the bullet and jump right into my husband's new hobby. We bought out first boat. It was a 23foot Aquarius. We both took the Coast Guard safety classes and enrolled the children in swimming lessons. We were ready to sail.

My mom had barely adjusted to us buying a house with a pool, and now this!! She was certain Barry's recklessness would one day kill us all. She never said a word to him, only to me. I did my best to explain to her that, in Miami, water was everywhere and we all had to learn how to swim and stay safe! I further reassured her by explaining the improvement over flying planes. In an emergency, I could not fly, but I could swim!

Nursing was my core profession throughout my life thus far, but after buying the house and realizing the money which commissions could bring, I decided to attend real estate school. During this busy time of settling into school for me and the kids, opening the practice for Barry, setting up our new home and sailing, we were constantly on the go. In the midst of all this, I was scheduled to have a change in birth control. Other than dealing with Barry being a bit of a selfish lover, like everything else, lovemaking was on his terms. Nevertheless, we definitely had spice in our love life. It seems we had both forgotten about the lapse in the birth control we had simply taken for granted over the years.

As my good fortune would have it, one evening Barry joined me for a shower and, amid love and passion, lo and behold, I became pregnant. Talk about excited, this surprise made my dream come true. I was ecstatic. Barry was a little worried that a new baby would interrupt his schedule. It took some reassuring, but he came around to realize that I would work things out, as I always did, and I believe he even enjoyed the newfound glow and happiness that the pregnancy brought me.

The nine months passed quickly. Then on Friday, June 28th at 1:30 AM, I gave birth to our 7 pound 9 ounce new baby daughter, Lisa Anne. When the doctor held her up I remember exclaiming "she looks just like me!" Barry and I were both excited and overjoyed to welcome our beautiful redheaded newborn into the world.

Having a new baby was totally rejuvenating. David and Tracy were now six and seven years old and were fascinated with the baby too. For Tracy, it was like having a new doll to play with and push in her carriage. So now I had three children. Close to my goal of four, but when I brought up the idea of one more baby, to Barry, I got a firm negative response.

By the time Lisa was born, I had my Real Estate license. She was already bringing me good luck. In my pregnancy, I was successfully busy selling houses and earning commissions. What did we do with the new income? We still had no furniture in our house, but we bought a bigger boat. Now we were up to a 30 foot Pearson, which we named Chapter 11. This boat was big enough to sail to the Bahamas, and that became our vacation destination.

Barry and I both became Ham Radio operators so that we could safely communicate ship to shore. Those were the days before cell phones, and ham radio provided safe communication from anywhere. Most every weekend we would sail in Biscayne Bay to Elliot Key, and when we could take a week off, we sailed to Bimini, Nassau and the Berry Islands. We were so lucky that the children were good enough to travel with, and that they accepted the many rules and strict discipline that was constantly being doled out by their father. They weren't always happy, because sailing meant they often had to miss their friends' birthday parties. As for Lisa, she was always content to travel with us. Have diaper bag, will travel!

The children were growing up beautifully. David was a serious A student and studying piano with a passion. A friend had arranged and paid for him to audition with Peggy Irwin, the area's leading piano instructor. She welcomed him into the fold and he was to go on winning first place in state piano concerto competitions. For his 13th birthday, I bought him a Yamaha Concert Grand piano. Up until then, he was playing on my old childhood upright piano. Tracy was doing great in school and following the family tradition of tap lessons, ballet lessons and gymnastics. She wanted no part of piano. Lisa did include piano lessons along with tap, ballet and gymnastics. My mom was so proud of them, as were we all.

During these years of 1977 and 1978 both my Aunt Bea and my Uncle Gil died of lung cancer. They were each 59 years old when they died, one year apart. As they were so influential in raising me and giving me the love of surrogate parents, when I was growing up, my world was once again shattered.

This time I fought the depression but did visit a psychiatrist who helped me understand the significance of these losses. They were the aunt and uncle who took over my care when my dad died and my mom seemed to disappear as she went off to work. They became surrogate parents and now I would mourn the loss of losing the "parents" once again.

Lisa, at four years old, told me she hated New Jersey because "New Jersey always makes mommy cry." It was clear that every trip to New Jersey was for a funeral. I never could afford to travel for the "fun" occasions, but somehow found the money to go to funerals. I had to make a personal pact to turn that pattern around!

Our combined incomes now gave us greater freedom to play. Our relationship was always stormy, but at the same time loving. That may seem impossible, but it was true. As long as the rules were followed, and kids were done with homework, fed and in bed by the time Barry was home, he had the quiet luxury of his wife and partner. This schedule had to be seem-less and perfect. My entire adult life, and to this this day, I still start each day with my "to do list" and feel guilty if I don't accomplish all I set out to do. While living with Barry, if one thing on my "to do list" was not done, he felt justified in furiously blowing up at me. Barry could be so cruel. Life was getting to be more and more difficult. My punishments were not physical, but rather emotionally abusive. Why didn't I leave? I was a victim, but I never thought of that as domestic violence. It was not until many years later that I recognized just how abused I was.

Barry became more and more rigid and demanding. His temper was probably worsened by the fact the he was beginning to hate the practice of medicine, and constantly talked of giving it up and just sailing.

No matter how many times I would apologize, he would refuse to speak to me over any minor infraction. That did not mean we did not make love. The bed was a separate issue. Even when he was not speaking with me, and I was begging his forgiveness for whatever caused his rage, all anger was to be put aside for the sake of sex. I used to tell him that it was like putting a bandaid on a cancer. But this was his method of dealing with me, and dealing with stress.

This pattern went on year after year. It was his way or the highway. If he said "jump", my response was to be "how high?" That was clearly the expectation.

The thread that runs thru this story is the fear and the agonizing guilt I carried throughout my life, my failure to be perfect. I tried so hard to be the best daughter, sister, wife, mother, nurse, and in general the best possible person. I tried, maybe sometimes came close, but I never was perfect and ultimately felt like a failure. The flashbacks haunted me at any time of day. Even while I was driving, I often found myself flashing back to that corner of my living room, just three years old, trembling with fear as the world around me crashed and changed forever. I literally never knew how I drove from point A to point B, because I was somewhere else, inside myself, in a dark and secret place.

I was deeply in love with my husband, but tortured by our relationship. I accepted his critical, punishing personality because maybe I felt I needed to be punished. As hard as I tried I could never make him as happy as I wanted to. I was a flawed personality. More and more, I sided with my children to protect them from Barry's anger. I vowed to myself that I could and I would always be their soft shoulder. I hate to admit that sometimes I would wonder to myself if I would possibly outlive him and have even a few years of peace. This was our pattern. This was how we lived over the next several years.

I enjoyed real estate, so I studied, took the exam, and passed to move up from a salesperson to a Real Estate Broker. I had run around enough selling homes and now was interested in commercial Real Estate. The hours would be much better for managing my home life. It made my brother so proud when I became part of his Real Estate Network. I opened my own Real Estate office and began to work for myself.

Barry was becoming increasingly disenchanted with the practice of medicine and more and more enchanted with sailing. December of 1980 he had an opportunity to buy an even bigger boat, a 41 foot Irwin Citation sailboat,

The Sea Owl. A cash deal would mean the best price, so he decided to take out a home equity loan to pay for the boat. Wanting to make him happy and being a dutiful wife, I signed the loan papers which created a second mortgage on our home, and we bought the boat. This was the end of 1980 and essentially the end of our marriage.

As we began the New Year, 1981, Barry announced he was ready to close his practice and "sail around the world". This was no longer talk, this was his plan. After all these years invested in Med School, Internship, Residency and becoming Board Certified in Ophthalmology, this was just incredibly unthinkable to me. Our beautiful children were now 13, 12 and 6 years old, just growing up, all in school and doing great. Our parents were getting on in years, and there was just no way I could separate from life and go sailing around the world. His solution was we could put the kids in a boarding school and visit them and our parents at least once a year. He was talking to Earth Mother. No way would I separate from my children. Not for him, not for anyone! He was furious with me!

I suggested he take a nice long sailing vacation. There were college students who would pay to charter a boat, with a captain, for a month long cruise. I was hoping that he could get this obsession out of his system. He liked the idea of just "getting away" but when he got back, he had only reinforced his plan to leave his practice.

CHAPTER 10

MY WORLD BEGINS TO CRUMBLE

My world was starting to crumble.   One day was worse than the next.   Barry became unpredictable and furious.   He would say he felt like he could just break both my arms, because I was being so difficult. These were just his words of fury.   He never touched me. There were weeks he wouldn't even speak to me, but expected me to carry on as wife and mother.   Trying to maintain our sex life was always like putting that band aid on a cancer.   Life began to unravel, he fully expected he could intimidate me into saying yes to his scheme.   But finally, I had said "no", I had found the inner strength to stand up to him.

One night, in bed, during our most intimate time together, he continued to give me an ultimatum that I was going to do as he said. I stood up for myself for the first time in my life. He was outraged, got out of bed and stormed out of the house. I frantically tried to run after him, begging for him to understand how impossible this plan was for me and our children. He was screaming at me that he "felt like a farmer who didn't like farming anymore." I was terrified but I refused to budge in my resolve to stay put. I was pleading that we could work things out, but he was beyond reasoning. He was saying "jump" and this was the first time in 21 years I did not say "how high".

When he left the house that night, in a fit of temper, he never came back to live there. He called constantly to try to convince me to change my mind. His exact words were that I had a choice. I could either stand on the boat with him and push the dock with my foot or stand on the dock and push the boat with my foot. Whatever would lie ahead, I was certain that I would always choose to stand on the dock, with my children, and push the boat with my foot. I felt like an amputee and had lost my stability. The rug had been pulled out from under me, I had lost my balance. I had lost my other half.

My world had totally imploded. I still am not sure how I managed to function during those months and years. I know I cried for the first three months after he left and pleaded, with him, for us to go to counseling and save our marriage. He refused. There was nothing I could do but literally beg him to stay and keep our family intact. He refused.

Telling the children that we were divorcing was something we did do together. After that agonizing discussion, Barry left the room and the house. David said he thought life would be better without him around. Tracy said whatever made me happier would make her happy, and Lisa said she couldn't understand why because "you never fight". Actually, she just never heard screaming, only days and weeks of the silent treatment.

I spoke daily to my brother for the strength which only he could give me. I was barely able to focus on the real estate business I was trying to run. I was an emotional basket case trying to juggle work and caring for my three children. My budget was shoestring. Being a struggling single mom and trying to put on a happy face for the kids was the biggest challenge. I would have to put tape over the holes in the kids' canvas sneakers, because there was no money to replace them. Thank goodness for hand-me-downs.

In a chance encounter, I ran into the nurse who had replaced my position with the plastic surgeons. We happened to cross paths in a medical office parking lot after taking one of my children to a doctor's appointment. Here it was 1981 and I had not seen Jackie since 1966. She asked what I was doing and when I explained I was going through the worst time of my life, in a divorce and raising my three children, she said she had a job for me. I would be a perfect home health coordinator. I didn't even know what that was, but Jackie insisted I come into the office the very next day. The company had a nurse leaving on maternity leave and needed an immediate replacement. She assured me that her boss would hire me immediately. That was what I did. I got the job and began my new nursing career in home health which carried me through the next thirty four years.

Even back at work in nursing and trying to keep the real estate business going, my checkbook would drop to 87 cents between paychecks. I was treading water for certain, but I did not sink.

After months of Barry's self-imposed exile, his brother suggested we get an attorney who could help us "settle matters" of separation. Somehow, he had arranged for the same attorney to represent both of us. That never worked.

After almost 3 years of negotiation hell, we had gotten nowhere. I was not even asking for alimony. My feeling was, if he wanted out, just let him go. BUT he should be responsible for his children. He would never agree on any temporary child support. Over those three years, he remained furious and blamed me for causing this nightmare just because I had refused to cooperate and get on the boat and take off with him.

He was constantly threatening. He threatened to kill me. He threatened to blow up our house because we were visiting with his parents for a holiday meal. In an attempt to calm him, they had to ask us to please leave and go home.

At the end of the three years of negotiation, court proceedings and no support, we were still in limbo, but it was actually hell. These were the days before the term "dead beat dads" laws were heard of.

I was somehow still in love with Barry and always hoping we could come to terms, until the last straw, one final court proceeding. Barry was demanding that my son's grand piano belonged to him. I had my original paperwork that showed the piano was purchased completely and directly by my personal real estate commission check. I ordered the piano and had it delivered on May 25th, my son David's 13th birthday. David's talent warranted this amazing concert grand. Shortly after the day I purchased it, Barry had told me that his accountant said if the paper work was in the name of his office practice that this could become some type of art investment and somehow create a tax deduction. I agreed, but fortunately, I had kept both copies of the purchase agreement. Going to court over his son's piano was the final straw! I told the judge that if Barry could find middle C on the piano, he could have it! The judge threw Barry out of court and my son kept his piano. THAT WAS THE DAY I FINALLY STOPPED LOVING MY HUSBAND!!

I guess at this point, I was at such loose ends and so distraught that my brother intervened and arranged for me to go to my own attorney and "get this divorce over with". The divorce was finalized in April 1984, after 21 years of marriage and three years after separating.

At Barry's insistence, at the time of divorce, he demanded I take back my maiden name. I would be denied any privilege as a doctor's wife. I was awarded full custody of my three children. He was given supervised visitation. Even though the terms were established: he gets the boat, I get the house, both equal in equity, and he was to pay minimal child support and provide insurance for the children. Simple terms. He paid nothing. He did nothing. My attorney's words were: "you can take a horse to water but you can't make it drink."

I was now forced to now hire a collection attorney. Having no money, I had to hire her using a contingency contract. She would only be paid from monies which she collected from him. She collected not one penny.

A few short months later, June of that year, in an overnight move, Barry closed his office, sold his practice, emptied our 401K account, bought supplies, running up our credit cards, got on his boat and left the country. His brother had helped him secure the proper paper work for taking the boat out of the country.

I only found this information out from a friend of mine, who was a patient of his. She had gotten a letter from his practice saying the office was closing due to a personal emergency. He had sold the good will and transferred all patient records to a local ophthalmology practice. When I got this information, over the phone, I drove over to his office building, only to look thru the window at empty rooms! Gone!

I went to the office to which his patient's charts were transferred to explain to the doctors the dire straits in which he had left our family. The docs explained he had taken a lump sum payment from them. Gone! I called the attorney, I called the sheriff. Delinquent child support, no 401K, no boat, and credit card debt, I had no choice. It was sink or swim.

The University of Miami threatened me with a lien on my home for Barry's delinquent student loans. I was forced to settle with them. The second mortgage, from the boat purchase now presented a lien on my home which, along with the first mortgage, became my responsibility, regardless of the divorce decree. It was financial disaster for me. I had already gone back into nursing to assure a paycheck at the end of each week. I was literally treading water from paycheck to paycheck. There was no choice but to become a survivor.

My son, David, used to tell me I should be angry and fight. Who would I fight? I explained that there are two types of energy, positive and negative. Anger is negative energy that is totally draining. And, since I was raising three children, I needed all the positive energy I could muster. Now that there was no father in the picture, I decided to have all the children share my name to show that we were a united family.

I know that my in-laws were very angry about the name change, but I was adamant that it never would have mattered had their father not abandoned us. I refused to buckle under. I chose to take the positive energy and be a survivor.

CHAPTER 11

SOME PEOPLE NEVER LEARN

S ome people never learn, and it seems I was one of those people. Barry had a close friend, Dave K, whom we both had met thru our ham radio hobby days. Dave built the radio towers for ham radio communications in Miami. He was a technician par excellence. Dave was a different, maybe an eccentric sort of personality, very self-boasting, very talented, and seemingly very wealthy. His core business was jewelry. He was a diamond dealer, a Rolex maven, an antique jewelry maven, an antique clock and watch maven, an antique gun collector maven, and a self-proclaimed expert at just about everything. He was always bragging about his talents and abilities. He was the socially annoying, boasting personality type. He dabbled in drugs, but "just socially."

Many of our professional friends dabbled as well. In the 70s and 80s it seemed that "dabbling" in drugs was common practice. Pot, cocaine and quaaludes showed up at social gatherings and I suppose were easily obtained. Barry and I did not dabble. There was a short time in Chicago we had tried to be sociable and "smoke pot" but it just wasn't our thing. As I had never even smoked a cigarette, I had a frightening coughing spasm and nearly passed out as I choked. Everyone else, including Barry, thought it was very funny.

Barry was attracted to Dave's fascinating personality and I was simply turned off by all his bragging. I considered Dave a pathological liar, but Barry reassured me that Dave was truly brilliant and talented.

Dave was married, supposedly living with his wife, but legally separated. He had one daughter. As the guys were best of friends, Barry invited Dave and his wife to go sailing with us. I was not feeling comfortable in Dave's presence. That day, Barry was his typical bossy self with me. He loved ordering me around to climb the mast, do boat chores and fix lunch for everyone. The next day, Dave called me to say I was the nicest person he had ever met and if Barry ever spoke to me that way again, in his presence, he would "deck him". I thanked him for his concern, but explained that was Barry's style, he was my love, he loved me and just always talked like that. End of conversation. I never told Barry that his friend had called me.

There were several years in the late 70's early 80's that Dave and Barry remained very close friends. And when that fatal day occurred, in March of 1981, when Barry stormed out of the house, the only person I could think of to talk some sense into him was his best friend, Dave. Somehow, Dave just slid into the role of our intermediary. To my knowledge, he tried his best to convince Barry to move back in with us and save the marriage.

Throughout this time, Dave spoke with me daily and listened to me cry and, with his words, tried to help mend my broken heart. I was grief stricken. I had to grow up without a father and all I ever wanted was for my children to have a father. Now my hopes and prayers were destroyed.

While my brother, Gerry, remained the steering current of my life and we talked long distance every day, Dave became my best friend. He was always there for me thru every crisis. If I couldn't sleep, I could call him at any hour of the night and he would talk me through the tears.

I remember the excitement in the house when he brought the children the pack-man game.   He would occasionally take us all out to dinner for a treat.   I had no money for treats.

Dave was always there for me, as moral support, when I went out on my first date three months into my separation. It had taken me three months to stop crying and decide I had to get on with my life.

Early on, I had interviewed with a divorce attorney who had called me, the next day, refusing to take my case because he felt he could become emotionally involved with me.   And indeed, three months after that interview, he became the first person I dated . I talked to Dave about how very weird I was feeling with a "new man" holding me, kissing me, and eventually making love to me.   Dave and I constantly talked about feelings. We soon found we could easily and comfortably talk about everything regardless of how personal. I used to say if I was catholic, he would have been my confessor.

Before long, Dave became MY best friend.   Strange how that transformation happened, but it did.   This man was a master at manipulating others.   Only many years later did I realize that, somehow, Dave had managed to discover my weaknesses and used them to position himself as my best friend.   I must have been blind not to see how he manipulated my life.   It is so true that hindsight is 20/20.

How or why could I turn someone I distrusted and disliked into my best friend and eventually my husband?

Dave played life like a chess game.   The longer I knew him, the more I understood his techniques.   He could see life five or six moves ahead.   There was always a plan that would work to his advantage.   Unfortunately, it is only hindsight that is 20/20.

Almost invisibly, without seeing it happening, I became his confidant as much as he became mine.   It seemed he needed me as much as I needed him.   What I did not realize at the time was that he really needed me more.   I never saw it coming, but one day, a couple years down the road, I realized I had fallen in love with him, he became my safety net, my security blanket, my best friend.   And so it goes, the story of my life.   I loved being needed.   I suppose I needed to be needed.   I was controlled inwardly and outwardly.

Becoming a romantic couple, I soon realized I could not tolerate Dave's "social drug use".   It became disgusting to me.   Since he wanted to live with me, after a major struggle, I was able to get him to quit drugs.   The struggle included dealing with his habitual lying and horrendous temper outbursts, like the time he smashed the windshield of my car because I caught him in a lie. You would think I had enough of temper tantrums. That outrageous behavior still was not enough for me to give up on him. We lived together for a while until I had to kick him out for continued lying and violent outbursts.

He bought his own house. Why I remained steadfast with him I cannot say. All I can say is that he made me feel safe. I guess my own personal struggles overtook my better judgment.

My mom became sick during this time. She remembered herself alone at age 38 with two children and now her daughter was alone at age 38 with three children. The stress I was going through was taking its toll on her mentally and physically. She fell, broke her hip and after it was pinned she was placed in a rehab. I visited her every single day. Dave was tolerant of my time with her in a way I knew Barry never would have been. For this tolerance, I was very thankful. I eventually moved her back to my house where she remained until she passed away.

As a single mom, those final years were a struggle, but I wanted her with me. Many years before, she and I had a conversation about parents growing old. I promised her I would never put her in a nursing home. I had to keep my promise to her, and I did.

Now she was gone. To me, her death was devastating. Since the age of three, she was my only parent. She was my lifeline. I could not imagine the world without her in it. Never did my world seem emptier.

I felt I was floating in space with nothing to ground me. I felt totally alone. I was the orphan I always feared I could be. Of course, I was old enough now not to need to have those thoughts about who would adopt me, but terrified at the emptiness I was feeling. Once again, I felt as if there was an actual hole in my heart.

I flew to New Jersey with my youngest child, Lisa, for her funeral. David and Tracy were in college and, as much as they loved her, there was no way I could afford to bring them to New Jersey to be with me. There was no money and I was too proud to borrow.

Their absence from that funeral still haunts me because she was such a loved and loving grandmother. Saying the final goodbye was another of the hardest moments of my life.

When I returned to Miami, I still could not and would not part with her hearing aids. I kept them safely in the drawer at the side of my bed for 2 years, thinking that if this was all only a dream, and not reality, she could come back and would need them.

Within the following year, I was still dating Dave on and off and began living with him again. Dave was a man that, I swore to myself, I would never marry. He had more baggage than I did. He no longer did any drugs, but he was a deeply scarred personality.

He was involved in jewelry estate purchases. His world was fascinating to me because his life was full of drama and beauty. I watched as he pored over estates of beautiful jewelry. He taught me an appreciation of antique jewelry, diamonds, and firearms, current and collectables. He took me to the range to do target shooting. I learned to shoot paper and he even had me shooting black powder rifles. He encouraged me to get my concealed weapons license, as Miami had danger around every corner.

I found myself carrying cash and jewelry to be delivered to other jewelers and merchandise to be sold to buyers for large sums of cash, which I was to carry back to Dave. I remember once being called to return the cash to the buyer because the watch they had bought was not genuine. It seemed I had become his gopher or his mule.

After dating Dave for 9 years, with that inner voice constantly telling me to avoid marriage, he convinced me I was wrong and we married. We had a private ceremony with a reconstructionist rabbi presiding. Although Barry was an atheist, he had refused to give me a "get", which is the Jewish document for a religious divorce decree that allows a woman to remarry. Just another obstacle he could put in my way. As the husband, he had all the control over that document.

Why did I marry Dave? I asked myself that question so many times. I tell myself it was because I felt alone. It was about safety. Dave would protect me from the threats of the world. My mom was gone. My children were all living away perhaps because they couldn't tolerate my relationship with Dave.

I was confused and vulnerable and struggling with life and with my emotions. My world was in a terrible state. My fears and my guilt and my flashbacks were always messing with my brain. I was needy. I needed to feel sheltered. I needed to feel safe. I needed to feel loved. I needed to feel needed. Excuses or reasons, whatever the case, I married him.

I knew my children were not approving at all of my choice of partners. It certainly hurt and made me sad, but I rationalized by saying they all lived away. They were living their own lives and I was certain I would have little input on their choice of partners.

Like an ostrich, I put my head in the sand and married him without even inviting the children to the wedding. I could rationalize that I could not afford to bring them to Miami anyway. No one except our witness couple attended the ceremony.

Later on, in the marriage, I was to learn from Dave himself, that what I craved in a relationship was Ozzie and Harriet, but what I got with him was Bonnie and Clyde. Life with Dave was life on the edge. A life tinged with paranoia, the exotic, the erotic and the dangerous.

Dave had mumps as a teenager and was sterile. He had learned, shortly after her birth, that the daughter he thought was his miracle, was not his biological child. This deception by his wife is the event which he blamed had caused all his emotional traumas. I blamed his drug usage.

I had never even met his daughter over the 9 years we dated. She did come to meet me after I married her father. I tried to recreate a bond between them, but that never worked. Too much water under the bridge to ever mend those fences.

As a couple, our schedules were completely opposite. I was always used to getting up at 6 AM, as the children were growing up, and now was working long hours to build my career in home health nursing. Dave was home and sleeping all day because he was a night owl. He liked to get up at 4 in the afternoon and get to sleep before 6 AM   Life was upside down.

My career provided him with stability, insurance, credit cards and a new legitimacy.   He seemed to be doing well.   The year after we were married, hurricane Andrew hit Miami. My house was destroyed.   Luckily, I had good insurance coverage and after 6 months living in a condo on Miami Beach, we realized there would be enough insurance money to buy a house on the island of Biscayne Point.   I sold the old house, "as is", without repairing the hurricane damage.

Our life together remained very isolated.   There were few friends, as Dave did not trust many people and didn't choose to socialize.   We had a few friends who were in business with him, otherwise we were just with each other.

A year after settling into our new home, was the night of the epiphany.   It was a night like any other night.   I had gotten to sleep before midnight.   I was a great sleeper. When I closed my eyes, the next thing I heard was the alarm clock.

On this particular night, I was startled awake before dawn by a male voice.   It was as if "he" was speaking right next to me.   That was the voice that said "you are me".   I felt as if I bolted awake.   No one was there besides Dave, who was sound asleep beside me. I just knew at that very moment that the voice belonged to my brother, Jackie, who had drowned when he was 5 years old. I tossed and turned and wasn't able to fall back to sleep after that. My mind was whirling. Did this mean I am the reincarnation of my brother? This is the thought was filling my mind and my senses. I will come back to the impact that night had on my life in an upcoming section of my story.

To continue telling about my life with Dave, I must say that his temperament was an ongoing source of struggle. It seemed to always be a tug of war between my time with any of my family and his time with me. He always wanted to dominate my time and keep my attention all to himself.

We had been married four years, when I got a call at work, from Dave's friend, Bob, at the pawn shop, telling me Dave had just been shot three times in a robbery attempt, and was being airlifted to Ryder Trauma Center. I should get there as soon as I could. Bob had no report on Dave's medical status.

I dropped my charts and ran from the hospital, where I had been at work reviewing cases. I ran to my car to get to him as quickly as possible. We were only about four miles away. The highway was backed up with stopped traffic. I pulled off the road and ran the last half mile to where he would be.

I knew he had carried cash that day to purchase jewelry from a woman whose jewelry he had appraised the previous week. It seemed she had him set up and, as he was entering the pawn shop, a car pulled up and someone began shooting at him. He pulled his own personal weapon out, but was unable to shoot his assailant. He said they were wearing bullet proof vests.

Dave had been shot in the shoulder, the stomach, and as his assailant approached and put a gun to his head demanding his cash, he hit at the gun and the last bullet went thru his knee. Our friend, the owner of the pawn shop, had set off a silent alarm and called the police.

When I reached the scene, the helicopter had already left for Ryder Trauma. I learned that the perpetrators were shot, caught and were also taken to Ryder Trauma by helicopter. I had to run back to my car and drive to the hospital where Dave was already being treated in the emergency room in preparation for surgery. After surgery and several days in intensive care, Dave had done better than I ever imagined and was discharged after 2 weeks with a colostomy and knee brace.

It was quickly apparent, he was deeply troubled emotionally as well as physically. As I searched for a psychologist for Dave, I found help for myself. My research led me to a psychologist who specialized in REM, rapid eye movement therapy, to treat Post Traumatic Stress Disorder. I interviewed her before bringing Dave in as her patient. She seemed wonderful, and the therapy very innovative. As we discussed trauma and Dave's situation, I told her of my flashbacks. She asked if I might like to see how this REM therapy worked. Of course, I agreed I would try. After just a few sessions, I was able to almost entirely eliminate the flashbacks and get rid of some of my guilt and fears. The process of revealing and reliving my flashbacks until they were erased was gut wrenching but the relief was nothing short of a miracle.

Dave was at home, but was anything but happy. He was depressed about the colostomy which would be reversed in the next month or two. He was furious and I think humiliated that he was victim to this crime.

He had routinely boasted about being a fantastic marksman and said there was always "a three second warning" when he would be able to draw his weapon and shoot an assailant. This time, he was proven wrong. He absolutely hated to ever be wrong. He would have fared much better psychologically had the morning newspaper read that "jeweler shoots and kills his assailants in self-defense during attempted armed robbery". However that wasn't the outcome at all. The good news was that he would recover from his physical injuries. The psychological injuries proved much more complicated. He just couldn't see any positive side, even knowing that he could have been killed or permanently bedridden.

I worked alongside his home health nurses and his physical therapists and did everything possible to bolster his spirits and turn him around to positive thoughts. He continued to grow more and more depressed, angry and anxious. I had found both a wonderful psychiatrist and psychologist for him. He was diagnosed with Post Traumatic Stress Disorder. The physical wounds continued to heal, but the psychological ones continued to magnify. He went for therapy. He was placed on any number of trials of antidepressants and antianxiety drugs. His anger and anxiety were reaching a peak. Nothing seemed to help.

As a nurse, I was not the least turned off by his colostomy, but he was totally devastated. He only had to wait a couple of months to have it reversed. This was longer than he expected but was necessary because he needed to be able to get up and walk after surgery to prevent further complications.

Life was a nightmare of tantrums and depression. He hated his doctors. He screamed with rage, he began to grab me and shake me out of desperation to be understood. I had to hire attendants to stay at home with him while I was at work. I was terrified as to what he would do if left alone. With medical and psychiatric treatment, we somehow persevered and tried to heal.

The case finally went to trial two years later. For both of us, reliving the crime in great detail was even more painful than I would have imagined. The outcome was that one of the perpetrators was sentenced to life in prison for shooting at a police officer and the other was sentenced to 25 years. I felt we had a victory in court. Nothing helped Dave. His anxiety grew worse.

Over the following six years, he remained continuously on medication, but grew progressively uncontrollable and aggressive. He had fits of screaming and made multiple threats of suicide. He kept his weapons close at hand at the side of the bed and under the bed. His psychologist warned me that he was unpredictable and could easily turn violent and kill me and himself. It was suggested that I have an exit plan for my safety.

It did finally come to that. The last night I was with him, he held his gun pointed at me while screaming at me to listen to him. He carried on this way until 4 in the morning. I was speechless. I was terrified. I tried desperately to calm him. I was alone with him and my thoughts were that I may not live to see the morning.

My alarm was set for 6AM to get up for work. When finally I calmed him enough to put down the gun and get into bed and try to sleep. I shut my alarm and when I was certain he was sleeping, I left the house as quietly and quickly as I could. I had packed some personal belongings in my car for just such an emergency. I got in my car and drove away. I was very thankful to have gotten out alive.

I had to stay in a hotel for several weeks until I could find a secure place to live. I was fortunate that my work kept me on the move all day so my whereabouts were never known.

My youngest daughter, Lisa, had worked for the State Attorney and knew some detectives. She arranged a police escort for me when I returned to the house to pack some of my belongings a few weeks later. Dave was escorted from the house, for just two hours, allowing me to go in and get my things out.

The nightmare was over. I remained legally married to him, just so that he would have continuity of medical coverage through my work until he was eligible for

Medicare at age 65. After leaving the house, I never saw him again, not even at the courthouse the day our divorce was finalized.

CHAPTER 12
LIFE CAN BE SHOCKING

Life can be shocking. The day began like any ordinary day at work.   That morning in January 1996, I was working at Baptist Hospital reviewing charts when I happened to run into Barry's past office manager, of many years.   It had been at least 12 years since I last saw Claire. That was in 1984 when Barry had closed his ophthalmology practice suddenly and within a day had left the country

I had since remarried and was managing to live my life.   My career as a Home Health Intravenous Therapy Coordinator was growing successfully and keeping me very busy.   My three children were all grown and living away.

When I spotted Claire, I went over to say hello and learned that she was there visiting her husband who was a patient. I offered to introduce her to my friends, the social workers, who could be of guidance to her with regard to her husband's care and discharge planning.

As a not so funny joke, I introduced Claire to them as my "late husband's" office manager. I said that because it seemed everyone had an ex, so I decided to be different. She looked shocked.   She took me aside and asked "how did you know?" I had no idea what she meant, so I apologized and explained the "late husband" humor. It seems that for these past 12 years, Claire had actually kept in touch, not only with Barry's brother, but with Barry himself, over all these years of abandonment.   She was quite a loyal ex-employee.   Much more than I ever would have expected or realized.

She went on to tell me that my brother in law had just spoken to her a few weeks earlier to say that Barry and his boat had disappeared after leaving the dock at Margarita off the coast of Venezuela headed for Ste. Maarten.   He never arrived in Ste. Maarten and after much investigation was now presumed pirated.   She told me the coast guard had been notified and their search had turned up nothing.

Of course, as soon as possible, I placed a call to my brother in law who verified the truth of Claire's story.   He said he had not called me because it was such troubling news and wasn't sure about wanting the children to find out. He went on to tell me that he and Barry had stayed in contact with one another over the past twelve years. A month or so earlier, Barry had asked him to send some supplies he was in need of. Wally was to ship them to Ste. Maarten as Barry was planning to return there within a week or two. He also told his brother he had invited an old friend, the divorced wife of a mutual friend, to join him for the sail. Obviously, they had spent some time together as a couple. For whatever my opinion was worth, she would have been the last person I could have pictured Barry being with. However, she had accepted his invitation and was flying to Margarita to meet up with him and join him on his sail.

Wally shipped the supplies as requested. Four weeks later he got a call from his contact on Ste. Maarten that the supplies had arrived, but Barry's boat had never arrived. He told me panic set in and he had immediately notified the coast guard of the situation. The dock at Margarita had confirmed the date he set sail. After weeks of investigation, he was told by the Coast Guard that there was nothing to report. They sent Wally a copy of their investigation proceedings. The sailboat had simply vanished. Wally had contacted the woman who was to have sailed with Barry and she said after flying to Venezuela and meeting up with Barry, she found the boat to be in disrepair and needing an icemaker. She decided not to join him after all, and she just flew back to Miami. Her decision may have saved her life.

You might think I could have cared less about what happened to my ex-husband. That is anything but the truth. I felt sickened. I would have much preferred to go on thinking how he had shirked all responsibility and was off on his lifelong vacation sail. The thought of him having been pirated was truly unthinkable. In fact, to this day, I still do not believe it is true. I actually believe he has simply taken off to foreign ports and is remaining incognito probably to avoid trouble with the law or the lawbreakers.

He was the father of my three children and we had a 21 year history together. Although the final 3 years were terrible, we had also shared a lot of love, and a lot of good times as well as our many struggles. A 21 year marriage has got to have lots of peaks and valleys

The worst part of this discovery was sharing the news with the children. Finding the right words to soften the presumed reality was very difficult. Their reactions were mixed. David said "well he lived like a pirate and died like a pirate". Lisa and Tracy were simply quiet and disbelieving. For the most part, we all were pretty speechless. How could life be so incomprehensible?   But this has been the story of my life and why I am writing to tell it.

I know I have been diagnosed with what is called "separation anxiety".   Saying goodbye is very traumatic for me.   I always fear that a goodbye could mean forever.   I do believe that life is just that unpredictable.   I have a hard time with "endings" and never can even remember the endings of movies or of books. When the curtain goes down or book is closed after the last page is read, I will draw a blank.

Over the years, it has troubled me that Barry's sister never spoke to her brother again after he abandoned me and the children.   She knew her other brother was enabling Barry to abandon his practice and his family responsibilities.   However, she was both angry and disappointed and intolerant of Barry's behavior.   Her decision not to speak with or placate him now was final.   There were no further opportunities to turn things around.   Both Bobbi and Ronnie have remained close to me and tried hard to preserve whatever family ties were left.

CHAPTER 13
THE EPIPHANY

The reincarnation epiphany which startled me awake that night, made major changes in how I felt about my life, past, present and future. The sound of that voice was so real and yet so hard a reality to accept.

I had never given much thought to reincarnation. If the subject ever came up, I might have casually said "I wish I could come back as a bird. To be able to be free and fly would be amazing."

Never in my wildest dreams did I think another soul could have entered my own. I was disturbed with the initial thought that I could be a reincarnation of a male.

But some remote part of my brain just knew this voice belonged to the brother I was born to replace. His life had been born again thru my life.

The pieces of my life just suddenly began to fit into place. My compelling desire to be near water, my terrifying fear of water, my unfulfilled father needs, my neediness throughout my life, my guilt, my obsession to bring happiness to my mother, my need to please my brother, and my struggles to always be good even perfect. From that very moment, in the middle of the night, I began to understand myself just a little bit better. I would lie awake until morning with my heart pounding and these thoughts streaming through my brain.

As early as possible, I called my brother, Gerry, and shared with him what had happened to me. Of course, he could only listen. No one but me could understand or accept the truth in what had just occurred. Did Gerry even believe in reincarnation? Did he think this was possible? Did he think I was crazy? In his typical, intellectual approach to questions, he calmly said: "listen, anything is possible. We have to keep our minds open to all sorts of possibilities." Nothing more, nothing less. My brother was the only one left to share anything else about our brother that had drowned. Yet he said nothing. My brother, who always had so many stories to tell, had no stories to share with me now. He was silent.

I am certain his life had also been drastically altered from that day going forward, but he chose not to share that part of his life. I had been the one to hear that voice, and I was the only one who could understand this bizarre reality and put the difficult pieces of my life together.

I would look at myself in the mirror and try to see any reflection of another soul looking back at me. Jackie was someone I never knew, so what was I looking for? Answers to questions? I would look at my reflection in the mirror and wonder for the rest of my life, but I never had any doubt that this was indeed my reality.

If I was searching for answers about myself, I had found those answers. I looked at pictures of my smiling family unit in 1939, before my birth. There was mother, father and two sons. I look at those pictures and think just how unthinkable that year would become. That unpredictable future no one can ever know.

My mom had passed away in 1988. I did my best throughout her life to eliminate as much of her stress as I could. Her happiness was my main concern.

But now the year was 2003. I became obsessed with the idea and finally decided I must become certified as a scuba diver. Terrified or not, this became my mission. I was going to face my greatest fear. The lessons were grueling for me.   I would have to force myself to stay calm, and breathe normally.   I was constantly fighting the urge to hyperventilate.   But I was determined to succeed. When I completed my certification, I would be able to dive with my brother in the forefront of my mind to help emphasize the beauty over the fear.   I would promise him that I would keep us safe.

CHAPTER 14
MOVING ON

Fast forward to 2003.

Leaving Dave was truly an escape. I left my house on Miami Beach before daybreak, with the few belongings I had prepared in advance. In anticipation of an emergency, I had already packed my licenses, my insurance policies, and some personal articles.

After weeks of hiding, I found a secure apartment on Brickell Key. I was 61 years old and finally ready to live my life and to overcome my fears. I began seeing a psychologist who approached me with what seemed like a startling therapy for my separation anxiety. She wanted me to write a series of goodbye letters. The first was to my father. The second was to Barry. And, of course, the third to Dave.

These were the hardest homework assignments I was ever faced with. But I did it. As I wrote, I cried as hard as I had ever cried saying goodbye to my father. I raged at the men in my life who had used and abused my love, and had stolen so much of life from me. But somehow, writing those letters brought closure and gave me a new freedom going forward.

My mom had passed. The children have long since grown and moved away. Now that I have accepted reincarnation as a reason for my strong fascination and yet stronger fear of water, I decided to bite the bullet and sign up for those scuba diving lessons as I had promised myself.

Overcoming fears is a process, and not an easy one, but my instructor was patient with me and eventually, after much encouragement, I became certified. I joined a dive group I had heard about through a nurse acquaintance. She and the group welcomed me. This group were all new acquaintances and all they knew about me was that I was a novice. They were very supportive and helped me with everything from choosing my gear to holding my hand as we began to dive together.

Being underwater was like an out of body experience. From the quiet stillness of hearing only my own breathing to the colors of the coral and that aquatic life that surrounded me, all these new sensations were absolutely thrilling. I thought of Jackie with every dive and every breath I took and promised myself I would stay safe.

I completely bonded with this group and within a couple of years, I had well over 100 dives, and was finally comfortable under water. I dove in Belize in the deep blue hole of Jacques Cousteau's explorations. I was lucky enough to have even been diving in Honduras with the whale sharks.

Out of this group of friends, one woman was willing to take a trip to Peru with me and climb Machu Pichu. Marla was twelve years younger than me. At age 64, I needed to challenge my physical stamina and Machu Pichu was the perfect choice. After flying to Lima and then acclimating to altitude in Cusco for two days, Marla and I were ready to climb on May 25th, 2005,. There were just the two of us and the sherpas we had hired to carry our heavy gear.

Climbing to elevations of over 13,000 feet was more difficult than I imagined. We stayed close to one another. With walking stick in hand, I climbed the narrow broken paths leading to our goal. There was a huge drop off the side of that path for much of the hike. It was a slow climb as I would have to catch my breath and wait for my heart to return to a normal rate time after time. We slept in our sleeping bags for 4 nights and at 4 AM the final morning began the climb to finally arrive and watch the sunrise over Machu Pichu. I have never had a more ethereal experience. Physically and mentally challenging indeed, but I did it!!

I am feeling I have entered the final years of my life. I am not at all afraid of that fact. I have accepted the fact that the life I have lived has been anything but ordinary. My children have grown up into wonderful people. I am so proud of who they have become after dealing with all the struggles we have faced together.

I am fulfilled in my job. Nursing and medicine have always been and continue to be rewarding to me. My job has become my career. I have a lot of responsibility which I gladly face each day.

I have escaped from control. I have escaped from danger. I have overcome my fears. I am alone and proud and strong and happy. I am in control of myself.

Whatever lies ahead will be OK. The future has to be better than what came before. Perhaps I have just become an optimist in my old age.

Three years on Brickell Key passed quickly.   After many meaningless dates, I am finding some comfort in a relationship with an old friend.   He is a retired physician, now living in Palm Beach, and we have known each other 25 years.   This rekindled friendship has grown into a love affair and potentially is leading to a permanent life together.   But there are warning signs.   This man is very controlling and I find I am feeling signs of that old stress. I have learned to remain in a self-protective mode.

It is hard to teach this old dog new tricks, but I am determined to stay strong.   Talk of marriage, of giving up my career to move and be with him are causing me continued stress and anxiety.   These are feelings I never wanted to feel again.   He is telling me that "it is written in stone" that we will marry.   That was just a statement not a proposal.   I was not asked how I felt about that.

How to say no to another controlling man is causing me a major problem.   I know I never want to go down that road again.   I definitely prefer to be living alone.   I had begun taking golf lessons and had become totally hooked. My gentleman friend as well as my intuition told me it was time to stop diving.   I had seen so much and had managed to stay safe, but I was not getting any younger, so I would move on to my next hobby.

Saying "no" has always been a problem for me. I am thinking that I might run off to Costa Rica when I retire. I have heard money goes a long way there and between social security and my limited savings, I could live out a good life alone. I know my children and I would visit me as often there as in Miami. And I know there is good medical care available in Costa Rica. This would be a necessity during those unpredictable senior years. This has become my future plan.

CHAPTER 15
2006

Now I fast forward to 2006. Dreams can come true in due time. My best friend, Judy, has been waiting to arrange a blind date for me with a gentleman she has known over 12 years. For over twenty years, Judy has been my soft shoulder, my confidante and companion. Her wisdom has always helped me remain strong throughout the traumas I have endured.

She has waited a year for the introduction because this man was widowed. But when the year ended, she made the call, gave him my number, and insisted that if he called me I should just meet him, and go out to dinner with him. Even if I was dating someone else, a dinner date would be harmless.   He called, and we set a dinner date which I almost cancelled because my daughter, Tracy, was in town for a surprise visit.   But, at Tracy's insistence, I went.

I chose a little Italian Restaurant, the Brasserie, which was just across the street. It was walking distance from my apartment, so that I didn't even have to get into his car. I could get this "obligation to my friend" over with.

January 27th, 2006, I sat across from the man who would become the love of my life.   I was so comfortable sitting across from BARRY 2.   Believe it or not, that was his name.   As we dined, we comfortably talked, laughed and even shed some tears.   That dinner lasted more than a couple of hours.   I don't remember noticing another person in the restaurant.

What was it about this gentle man that made him different from all others?   We walked back across the street to my condo building and said goodnight with a little kiss.   The next day, when Judy inquired, I had to admit that if he called me, I would go out with him again.   She told me he said the same thing.   It wasn't so much "chemistry", as the "comfort" of that first date. On our second date, it certainly felt like chemistry between us, and by the third date, I was certain that was the case.

On that second date, we went to an opening at Sea Aquarium. The weather was cold and windy. Barry stood behind me and put his arms around me to shelter me from the cold. I had never felt such tenderness or warmth from a man. It was a sort of a magical feeling. At the movie theatre that night, it was still cold. Barry placed his jacket over me, and to this day I can remember the feel of that jacket.

By our third date, we both felt such a connection, being with one another, we talked about making this a monogamous relationship. Along with the safe sex talk, we discussed the fact that no matter how the relationship progressed, I would never marry again, and he was OK with that. Marriage was not what either of us was looking for. That discussion out of the way, we were more than ready to take the next step. I can stop right there. We were perfectly compatible and very much in lust, though that love word never came up for over a year. I will admit right here that I am the one who said it first. It was a brave, but uncontrollable step when the moment was right.

Our relationship began in January 2006. I have never been happier in my life. We lived only 12 miles apart, but after dating for 5 years we were both tired of fighting the traffic so we decided to try living together. That decision to cohabitate was really only because of the miserable traffic in

Miami. But, living together proved very easy and very comfortable. Our patterns and personalities were well matched.

In April of 2011, on a birthday cruise for Barry, aboard the Celebrity Eclipse Ship, Barry proposed. I felt something was wrong, and feared the worst, when he asked me to come sit down on the balcony for a talk. Out of the blue he asked if I would marry him. I wasn't sure what I heard him say, so I must have said "what"? His next words were "I'm asking you to be my wife" and, I think, without a moment's hesitation, my answer was YES.

I have loved this man in an entirely new way. He has taught me a new meaning to the word love. Our relationship, our devotion, our love and our life together is indescribably easy and natural.

Our wedding was on January 6th, 2012. Just about 6 years from the day we met. It was a beautiful celebration with 50 of our closest friends and family. Our honeymoon was joined by our children and grandchildren and dear friends Ian and Linda who felt they just had to bear witness to this event.

Don, along with Judy, our matchmaker and witness, will be forever loved and, of course, also remain our friends for life.

Friendships have blended.   Our lives have blended. Our families have blended and we are looking forward to growing old together and sharing every day we are given.

I will never take this life or my husband for granted. I shall count my blessings every day.   And, by the way, we changed his name to Barry 1.